SCARRED

THE TRUE STORY
OF HOW I ESCAPED
NXIVM
THE CULT
THAT BOUND
MY LIFE

SCARRED

SARAH EDMONDSON
WITH KRISTINE GASBARRE

CHRONICLE PRISM

Library of Congress Cataloging-in-Publication Data available.

ISBN: 978-1-4521-8426-5 hardcover
ISBN: 978-1-7972-0146-7 ebook

Manufactured in the United States of America.

Interior design by Pamela Geismar.
Typesetting by Maureen Forys, Happenstance Type-O-Rama.
Cover design by Sara Schneider.

10 9 8 7 6 5 4 3 2 1

CHRONICLE PRISM

Chronicle Prism is an imprint of Chronicle Books LLC,
680 Second Street, San Francisco, California 94107

www.chronicleprism.com

To my beautiful boys—
you have taught me what love really is.
I hope one day, when you are old enough,
you will read this and be proud of your mama.

And to my husband, who made me laugh
and find light in the darkness.

I love you all.

AUTHOR'S NOTE

This account is filled with friends and associates with whom I shared key moments and experiences during my twelve years in NXIVM.

Because of the federal case that has involved some of NXIVM's senior executives, or simply due to their personal preference to no longer be associated with the organization, some of those closest to me from this era of my life have requested not to have their names mentioned in this story. With my whole heart, I honor their wishes.

I also apologize to those who would have preferred to have remained anonymous but who have already been named in headlines in connection with my story. I have worked to protect your privacy, but because of the media attention around this case when I came forward and went to the FBI, I could no longer inform the narrative.

This story has been rendered to the best of my memory in the wake of these traumatic events. Some quotes have been reconstructed but always reflect the true essence of what was said, while other conversations and accounts were taken directly from the thousands of documents, videos, and audio files that we senior coaches in NXIVM were required to keep over the years.

As I work to regain my personal power and move past what happened, there's a special message I have for the friends and people close to me whom I became distant from or lost contact with over the years I was a proponent of NXIVM's practices: I'm deeply sorry. I'm working to start again. Hopefully my actions and all that I share in this book will be a step toward making amends as I begin to repair the impact my twelve-year journey had on those around me.

CONTENTS

SCARRED

THE SCAR

It's fading now
Reminds me that he never owned me.

Their silence.
Erodes the memories of our friendship
And leaves me naked.

Where was I before I met you?
Floating and eager
Too young to catch the flags.

My heart.
Open and pure.
I have love around my neck.

"Me too."
Their voices merged around me.
And held my hand so I could speak

Before I leave to heal
I plant barbed wire between us.
And wrap myself in cashmere sheets.

I'm back.
Ready for the leaves to turn
To start again.

Sarah Edmondson
Fall 2017

THE INITIATION

MARCH 9, 2017

"Go into the guest room and get naked."

I stare at her—my best friend, Lauren Salzman—as we stand inside her home. She was the maid of honor in my wedding; she's the godmother of my two-year-old son. She's been my closest confidante for the decade-plus that I've been involved with NXIVM, the person I would go to with my most personal challenges . . . but our relationship changed instantly just over a month ago when I accepted her invitation to participate in this "secret circle of women," who, as I'm about to learn, have all been recruited from the inside. We would fight to improve the world with our strength, she said, and hold each other accountable to our highest self-actualization. It was the women's empowerment I was looking for through a secret society, just like men have in organizations like the Masons. Yet from the moment I committed, I felt she'd been taking things a little too far.

Naked?

Any resistance would be turned around and used as my issue. It would prove that I'm "entitled," or Lauren could say that I'm "mad-dogging," NXIVM's term for being defensive. Still, I can't help searching her face for more explanation. *Why?*

"Sarah," Lauren says, "you have to get over your body issues."

But my uncertainty in this moment has nothing to do with my body image. From all my time in this organization, I know this is how

NXIVM works: anytime you question your coach's instructions, even if you totally disagree with what they're saying, they twist your reaction and cause you to doubt your natural response to question your own sanity.

Later I'll understand that this was the structure to support the gaslighting method that has trained me away from adhering to my instincts throughout my twelve years in NXIVM. So instead, I listen to Lauren. "It's just me, and women you know," she says, as if to make me feel more at ease, and closes the door.

I stand frozen for a moment after she leaves, aware of my body's last-ditch attempt to protect my well-being and dash out that door. The hardwood floor creaks beneath my toes as I shift my balance to remove my jeans. Goosebumps radiate across my skin when I lift my top over my head and cradle myself in the cold.

Lauren invited me to this initiation ceremony to meet the group of women she referred to as my new "sisters" for the first time. But I don't know who will be present when I enter, apparently *naked*, or what we'll be expected to do. Lauren said we'd all be receiving an identical tattoo the size of a dime—that we'd all share. I've never wanted a tattoo. As a wannabe hippie teenager, I'd briefly considered a Celtic knot, then later, in my early twenties, a Wonder Woman emblem. I've always been glad that I held off, as those symbols were merely passing phases, not a lifetime commitment in my personal style. But now, wearing nothing, I take a seat on the bed and trust that this initiation process has been designed to bond us together as an elite squad of women. This tattoo represents my commitment to this mission, *our* mission, which is not a passing phase, but a lifetime commitment. *We must raise all others as all others raise us.*

Each time I've recited this part of NXIVM's twelve-point mission statement, I've proclaimed my ongoing commitment to improve myself in my effort to be at-cause in our world, taking full responsibility as the generator of every single experience in my life. Lauren has guaranteed that nothing could equip us with more strength than being initiated into this sisterhood. From what she says, this will be true empowerment.

Her guest bedroom is small and bright, the March afternoon sun surging through the windows and simultaneously highlighting my body for scrutiny. It was almost three years ago that I gave birth, and I've returned to my pre-pregnancy size—but standing naked inside someone else's home, I view my parts in imperfect fragments, like a stranger might. I examine the varicose veins on my legs, my uneven breasts, the little pouch on my belly that was washboard-flat before I had my son. As I sit gingerly on the bed, I hear Lauren's footsteps on the stairs—and then someone else's. I realize I've just pulled the duvet off the bed to cover myself. *Who is with her?*

Then the questions flood over me:

What is this?

Where am I?

How did I agree to this?

Just go with the flow, Sarah! I tell myself. Lauren is your best friend; *you can trust her.* I've known Lauren for twelve years. I remind myself: *You're safe with her.*

For years the NXIVM coaches whom I've worked with have encouraged me to make an effort to overcome what they call my "control issues." If I don't go along with this, Lauren will say that I'm failing at my commitment to move past this because right now, I'm being controlling. This day is about to teach me the power of the training I've received, and how successful the program has been at silencing my own inner voice.

As I listen for more movement from the hallway, my senses absorb everything with hyper-awareness. More sounds on the staircase. An unrecognizable female voice in the hallway. The echo of a door closing in one of the nearby bedrooms. I've been in this house a dozen times, but today everything feels different. The heavy, dark wood trim. The thick velvet duvet. This is an old house—since I've known Lauren, I've always been struck at how her home feels so full of history. *What are we doing here?* I ask the ceiling. It hangs over me in an indifferent silence.

The space seems strange to me, and so does Lauren. As the head of NXIVM's education path and one of the company's most influential senior leaders, she's known for standing authoritative and at ease. But when she pokes her head back inside the bedroom, somehow she appears so small. "Put this on," she whispers, handing me a black piece of cloth. "Come take my hand."

Go, Sarah. I peel myself from the bed and fumble to tie my blindfold, feeling like a preschooler getting ready to be spun around by the teacher before taking a swing at a piñata. I think of my son.

Stripped of my sight and my clothes, I slowly feel for the curve of Lauren's palm before I slip my hand inside it. As she leads me through the hall, I recall the way she'd stressed that we each were required to arrive promptly, exactly fifteen minutes apart. Her strategy was that none of us recruits would bump into each other before the big reveal.

Lauren starts down the stairs and I follow, one unsteady step at a time. The careful choreography is my first hint of just how high the stakes are for her. Even when she greeted me at her front door, she seemed apprehensive, speaking in a low voice in a way that told me there were a lot of details that had to go just right. "Welcome," she'd whispered. "It's so good to see you. I can't believe this is actually happening." In time, all the nervousness would make sense.

We move across what my feet identify as the linoleum floor in her kitchen, then through the foyer and into the adjacent sitting room. She'd had me remove my watch with my clothes . . . but by now, I worked out, it had to be about midafternoon. My blindfold was nothing more than a thin black napkin, most likely from the former Italian restaurant that NXIVM's resident heiress, Clare Bronfman, bankrolled to serve as the company's exclusive, members-only clubhouse. In the organization, we all refer to the venue by the name Apropos. NXIVM's executives chose the spot for its location, just a four-minute drive from the Albany, New York, suburb of Clifton Park—home to our founder Keith Raniere and the upper ranks of his team, including Lauren.

Physical proximity is crucial to Keith, and all the women who work as senior-level coaches in NXIVM's headquarters live nearby: Lauren; her mom, Nancy (the president of NXIVM); Allison Mack; Nicki Clyne (whom I enrolled shortly after I joined twelve years ago); and over a dozen more. Keith and the community don't occupy a commune per se, but they live intentionally within walking distance of one another in a small condominium development. Lauren's house sits between the neighborhood of Knox Woods and the hamlet where her mom lives.

The condo that my husband and I rent is thirty minutes away in a different suburb. The decision for him and me to maintain some distance from the community had generated tension between us when we were looking for a condo to rent for when we needed to fly in from our home in western Canada. I had wanted to find a place that would be close to my friends, while he was seeking a property that would give us a little privacy, away from our colleagues, along with easier access to the airport and train station. In the end, his points made the most sense, so we wound up renting a condo in another suburb.

As my feet find themselves on the sheepskin rug in Lauren's living room, it occurs to me that my husband feels so far away. I find myself missing him, even though it was only a while ago that he dropped me off here for what Lauren had instructed me to tell him was just "a meeting."

Lauren guides me to sit on the rug and be still. I sense that there are people on either side of me. We wait, though I'm not quite sure what we're waiting for. I'm not sure if they do, either. I've never been naked with any group of people, certainly never while I was blind-folded without knowing who was present. It feels like standing in a police lineup before a one-way mirror. This wasn't the first time that being a part of NXIVM made me feel as though a team of people were viewing me from some hidden angle, determining my fate.

I hear more footsteps come down the stairs, through the kitchen and foyer, and into the room to join us. In this eternity of time, I can hear the breathing of the women around me as our collective anxiety builds. None of us, including Lauren, have any idea that today is the beginning of the end of NXIVM.

Next to me, someone clears her throat. Someone else giggles. Then we all laugh, a shared case of the jitters rippling throughout the room. A quiet relief settles among us that at least the bodies surround-ing us are all women, and all friendly.

"Relax, ladies," I hear Lauren say. There's a feigned grandiosity in her voice. "You all know each other. Now: take off your blindfolds and meet your sisters!"

Again, I'm like a child when I take off my blindfold for my eyes to locate Lauren, who's positioned herself above us, atop a chair.

Candles flicker on the floor near the rug as Lauren reads from her computer to deliver a few formal lines of address like we're receiving some great privilege . . . but as we all glance around at each other, the tension is palpable. *Why is she reading this from her computer?* I wonder. *Wouldn't she have printed all this out for what she's described as such a momentous ceremony?*

Lauren had been correct in saying that I know every woman here. There are five of us, including myself. Two are colleagues who have flown in from California; the other two traveled from Mexico. I flew into town for this meeting, which would be followed by the tenth eight-day Jness (pronounced "juh-NESS") training that we've taken in four years with a core group of devoted seekers, aiming to elevate our consciousness about feminine power and male-female relationship dynamics.

But nothing about this current experience feels elevating. The Mexican women wrap their arms across their chests. One of them recently gave birth to her third child and appears very uncomfortable sitting fully exposed among us. She and I are the only ones in this circle who have children, and I regard her in this shared bond. But while she's typically confident, she appears very uncomfortable in her body—her stomach still a little stretched out, her breasts engorged and swollen. I recognize her pain in sitting here . . . and I feel it myself. I tuck my knees up in front of me, my toddler coming into my mind again. The vulnerability of this experience reminds me so much of what it must feel like to be a child. "You need to get over your body issues, ladies," Lauren says. She will continue to repeat this throughout the afternoon.

What happens next I will later strain to remember, my mind spinning so. My thoughts vacillate between figuring out some excuse to back out and leave, and trying to calm myself. Lauren continues to read from her computer, weird words that sound like ancient scripture; something about gurus and disciples. She describes how DOS will work—that's what Lauren has called this group, pronounced simply *doss*—now, she says, that we're officially in a "circle" together. She explains that she's our master now, and our task is to serve her, support her, and help her with her mission. We will learn to be less self-involved as we focus our attention on "other." This, she says, is the ultimate spiritual exercise. And just like what we've all learned for years through NXIVM's Executive Success Program (ESP) curriculum, we will feel uncomfortable. She will push us, but if we stick with it, we will grow in ways we can't even imagine yet. This is her pledge in return for ours. Finally, she says, the collateral she has collected from each of us—the bank account details; the photos of us in which she instructed some of us to pose nude while simultaneously displaying our faces and our labia; the videos where we confessed our deepest, darkest secrets—would ensure that we would never, ever give up on reaching for our highest potential. To have that damaging information on the line will assure we all stay on "the path."

Lauren dismisses us for a brief break to get dressed, and instructs us to reconvene in a few minutes for a potluck dinner. As I get up, I watch her take down her iPhone, which I realize had been propped up on the mantel of the fireplace behind us. We're used to being video-taped in trainings; in fact, Keith and Nancy have a library full of video and audio files that they've maintained over the years. But I've never known them to videotape us in secret . . . and certainly not when we're naked.

Had Lauren filmed that whole thing?

Nah. Couldn't be. That would not have been cool. Not without our consent.

I've brought premade butternut squash soup from a nearby Whole Foods as my contribution to the potluck. All of the women carefully measure out their portions: a half-cup of soup, a small plate of salad. They're calorie-counting, a NXIVM practice that I've always refused to follow. They called me "decadent" when I would savor an entire avocado with my lunch, glare at me over their zero-calorie miracle noodles, fat-free yogurt, and baked squash. I would find out later that Keith liked his women at around one hundred pounds and demanded that they stay thin.

After we eat dinner, we all pile into Lauren's BMW and follow her instruction to put the blindfolds back on. Then she shares that she will drive us to the "secret location." I wonder what people on the street will think if they see a car driving by, carrying five women all crammed into the back seat and wearing black blindfolds. There's so much that makes me question the judgment of whoever organized this whole thing. *It's all women you know*, Lauren had said when she invited me in to join DOS back in January. She explained that this would be a lifetime commitment to one another. That part was the least challenging aspect of my willingness to commit to this, as I had always imagined being Lauren's friend for life. For years we've joked about growing old together and doing trainings for NXIVM into our senior years. I've trusted her implicitly . . . but this night is so bizarre. I've never been in a sorority, but I've seen enough movies to know what hazing and initiations are about. My guess is that this undertaking had to have been started by some of the young women who have relocated here permanently over the years. They're the ones most likely to consider themselves close enough friends to make this lifelong kind of pledge to each other.

I try to follow the route in my head as we weave through the maze of Knox Woods, Lauren driving for so long that, beneath my blindfold, I can sense that the sun's going down. I believe it's just past dusk as she slows the car to pull up to our destination. She must have been killing time waiting for the darkness to fall.

We take each other's hands in a line, one leading the other while we're all careful not to trip. "No talking, ladies," Lauren says. As we navigate our steps in silence, I'm pretty sure from the familiar carpet as we make our way inside that I know where we are: this is the home of Allison Mack, a modest ranch-style house that sits on a corner in the heart of Knox Woods. My guess is confirmed when we make our way farther into the house and from under the bottom of my blindfold I can see the feet of ornate furniture. Allison's taste has always been . . . unique. Just like everything in her life, her furniture is special— opulent, elaborately patterned, gilded with gold and silver. Boho-royal chic. The scent of perfume hangs in the air: Lily of the Valley. Floral, pungent, with a distinct staying power.

After Lauren has filed us into the guest room and closed the door, we're allowed to take off our blindfolds. She tells us not to leave, unless we need to use the restroom—but if we do, we have to put our blindfolds back on to step across the hall so that we can't identify where we are.

Lauren tells us to strip again, this time down to our underwear. I don't know yet that within minutes, this room will lose its chill as we'll be sweating in panic and pain.

My attention turns to the windows, observing that the blinds have been drawn. Slowly, I take in the rest of the room: it's been set up with a massage table, a couch, and a chest. There are no decorations on the walls, and the only light is harsh and fluorescent. From her computer, Lauren reads more about our mission as members of DOS. Then Dr. Danielle Roberts enters—a petite woman, the resident female doctor in the NXIVM community. She'd taken close care of one of our mentors, Pam Cafritz, in her battle with renal cancer before Pam passed away four months ago. Keith had also recently named Danielle the new face of the recently launched exo/eso training, which was a yoga- and Pilates-inspired fitness curriculum. Danielle had recently split from her boyfriend, even though they'd joined ESP—NXIVM's Executive Success Program—together.

There's a doctor here to administer the tattoos, I think. If I'm finally getting one, at least it will be safe. It's at this point that Lauren peels back the button of her jeans and slides her underwear down. *What IS that?!* Before I can catch myself, this is the first time I'll outwardly protest. "That is not the size of a dime, Lauren." And it certainly isn't pretty, as she'd promised it would be when we discussed this two months ago in January when she came to visit me in Vancouver immediately following Pam's funeral. The others gather around, studying the mark.

Lauren is flustered. "It fades!" she says. "It turns white." A white tattoo? That sounds hideous—but as I examine hers closer, I think white would be the more attractive choice. Her mark is raised, red, and inflamed, like a hunk of meat hanging from one of the most delicate places on her body. "It's a symbol for the four elements," she assures us, and her words grow foggy in my ears as she says something about the seven chakras. One of the other women says she thinks it's Latin. I can only think of my husband. What will he make of this? When we're in bed and this raw symbol is an inch from my private area? Did Lauren really think I'd be OK with this?

Inside, I'm freaking out, but I think of what I have been working on with my coaches. *Sarah, you're just looking for the back door. What they've taught us is right: breaking commitments is what women do. This is what makes you weak. You are strong! You can do this.*

And I remind myself of what this means within NXIVM. *You're the only green sash here besides Lauren*, I remind myself. I'm one of the highest ranking in the whole company.

Just as I'm contemplating this, Lauren pulls me aside. "You need to show the others how to do this," she whispers.

You're the example for these other women, I tell myself. *Be a badass.*

Before the ceremony, they give us a stencil to trace the shape of the symbol onto our bodies. We're told to make sure it's hidden beneath our panty line so we can wear bathing suits without exposing our secret mark. A couple of other women in my group take turns holding the stencil in place for each other. On my own, I trace it, taking some comfort that this part is not permanent, yet.

Then they tell us to remove our underwear as they call Gabriella, a high-level coach from Mexico, to go first. Gabriella helps to run a center like the one I run in Vancouver and has been working to reach the coveted level green in her training. As I watch her step forward, I'm sure she knows that this initiation is a big part of getting that promotion. No one ever gets the go-ahead to advance in the company without Lauren's blessing. Lauren pulls me aside and whispers: "Gabriella's so indulgent, look at her body!" I glance over her shoulder at Gabriella, whose curves I've always admired. I look back at Lauren in her trademark draped tunic top over boy-cut jeans. In a flash of conscience, it occurs to me that she's so often guilty of what NXIVM forbids us to do to others—specifically, gossiping. If this is supposed to be an empowering exercise, why is she criticizing Gabriella's body?

I don't know yet that Keith is a player in this, or that what Lauren really means is that this DOS recruit has some work to do before she'll be Keith's type.

Lauren turns on the video camera on her phone and hits Record. I remind myself that it's OK, that Lauren is like family. I've gotten used to being filmed at trainings and other NXIVM events—they say it's so that what Keith and Nancy say is never misinterpreted, and for the library of documents they keep that contain records of Keith's wisdom. Lauren had told me that all the materials related to this women's group would be stored inside a locked vault that only she had access to. *You can trust her.*

Gracefully, Gabriella climbs onto the medical exam table. I can smell rubbing alcohol even as I hover by the wall when Danielle wipes the area on the left side of Gabriella's pubis with disinfectant. "I'm going to touch your skin with this," Danielle tells her, "so you'll know how hot it will be." Lauren nods us toward the table, her subtle way of suggesting that we each hold down a body part so Gabriella won't be able to move and mess up the fine lines as Danielle works.

I move in and take a place at Gabriella's feet, teaming with one of the women from California, who takes her other foot. Lauren passes around medical masks for us to wear, which I surmise is for hygienic purposes so we're not breathing germs over Gabriella's mark. I look around, observing how strange this is. Apart from the masks, all of us, except Lauren and Danielle, are standing here unclothed.

When the iron first makes contact to her skin, Gabriella's whole body flips and tweaks, as if she's being electrocuted. She screams out in pain. Above her surgical mask, the woman holding her other foot meets my eyes, a distinct transaction between us: *What in the actual fuck?!*

I can't pull my attention away from Gabriella's pain. It's a horror movie now. I realize that they've given us the masks because the instrument Danielle is using, an electric surgical device with a live tip, is actually burning Gabriella's flesh. The smell of scorched skin filters through the mask, into my nose, to my stomach. I close my eyes and position my nose tightly against the skin of my shoulder.

Lauren takes me to the side. "See how weak and indulgent she is?" she whispers. "You have to show them how to do it. It's really not that painful."

The minute specifics from here on in will cluster in my mind because of the sensory overload I'm trying to process. After probably 45 minutes, Gabriella sorely slides down from the table and another woman climbs on board without hesitation. This obedience is not surprising; for years, they've coached us that if we feel the "urge to bolt," as they've always called it, that's our evidence the program is working. We have been trained to ignore our discomfort. I know that it's too late when they call me for my turn.

I've tried to work it out: how could I get the hell out . . . and to where? Should I call my husband to pick me up? He's watching our son at our condo thirty minutes away. The collateral they've collected hanging over me like a gun to my head. I recorded a video saying something untrue and horrible about every member of my immediate family. They're holding that material, and I watched as Lauren texted it off somewhere when she first came to pitch this initiative to me. I don't know who's seen it—only that they would release it publicly. I had taken a vow of obedience with Lauren, and that collateral is a guarantee that I'll keep my word. *Am I strong enough?*

I'm focused on proving myself in this ceremony. For years, they've been training us for this: to become a highly evolved, self-aware group of women who are agents for moving the world forward. And like Gabriella, I know that any promotion in the company where I've worked for twelve years will hinge on how I behave in this moment. Technically, I have a choice, but I certainly don't feel like I do. The knowledge of all this, combined with the fear of the collateral being released—mostly of my family seeing those wretched videos where I spewed lies about them—tips my decision. If I just lie still, I tell myself, it will all be over soon.

It won't be until months later when the *New York Times* story breaks and I read another branded slave's account that I'll remember we had been instructed to say: "Master, would you brand me? It would be an honor." From the second I climb onto the table, acutely aware that I am lying in the sweat of my sisters, I will have blocked that out. Lying there completely naked, I am at my most vulnerable but determined to prove my strength. I try to keep my legs closed as my body wills itself to protect my most private area. Both to avoid moving and to keep my body from revealing how vulnerable I feel, I tell myself: *I am a warrior. I birthed a human. I can handle pain.*

But nothing could have ever prepared me for the feel of this fire on my skin. Danielle drags the pointed ember like a needle-tip match across my skin in the most tender, sensitive area of my body. I clench, recalling the feeling of elastic bands being snapped against me when I got laser hair removal on my bikini line years ago. It seemed like such a barbaric thing to put myself through at the time. This is so much worse.

Lying here now, I can feel each millimeter of my flesh singed open. I close my eyes and imagine staring into the face of my son. I think about the moment he came into the world after the hardest part of my labor, when he was crowning and I could reach down and touch the top of his little head as I encouraged him to join us. I connect into my love for him; I concentrate on the miracle of birth. I use the tools from this program to "change my state," as we say in NXIVM, into one of utmost love and joy as I try to transcend the pain.

I am not sure if I was actually feeling some sort of transcendent emotion or if I was dissociating out of my body. Either way, between each line of the symbol, Danielle stops to let me recover while Lauren takes these moments of peace to read more from her computer. *Just finish this thing!* I want to scream. But Lauren continues, instructing me to repeat by rote, and then Danielle begins her work again. I don't know the exact time it takes. I only know that mine goes the fastest because I somehow managed not to let myself squirm or fight it.

When the last line's been drawn, my eyes need a moment to adjust to the light. I feel like I'm floating out of my body. Lauren's face comes into focus as she looks down at me lovingly, showing great pride. My sisters, who'd all been cheering me on, move in to grip me as I come off the table. *I've done it,* I think. *I'm a warrior. If I could do this, I can do anything.*

Lauren asks me to take her phone and videotape the woman whose turn is next. As I'm filming, I notice a text come through—

KAR

How are they doing with each other?

At first, I ask myself: Who would Lauren store in her phone as KAR? I search my mind for anyone we know named Karen—is that Karen, an actuary in NXIVM who's done a lot of software programming for the company?

Then a fleeting thought: *Was that Keith?* If Keith knows about this, I tell myself, then he's going to know that I just nailed that challenge. Lauren will tell him how strong I am, and he'll realize more than ever what an asset I am to his team.

That thought passes when I remember Lauren said this was a group for women, by women. There's no way Keith would be involved in any way.

These initials will become an important clue that nothing about this ceremony—in fact nothing about NXIVM as I've known it—is what I've been taught to believe.

I'll also find out that Lauren had indeed recorded all of us naked inside her living room, that Danielle was alleged to be one of the many women in Keith's private harem, and had accepted the role of branding us for DOS. I'll discover that this entire branding ceremony was constructed to serve as the ultimate "trauma bonding" to connect us five women with one another for life. (This sadistic type of conditioning is classic Keith Raniere methodology.) I'll learn how they were bringing me in to recruit young women whom they would coerce to have sex with Keith.

This mark is not only a physical injury. Soon, a therapist will help me to understand that it is what's known as a "moral injury," a permanent trauma to my conscience as I discover the true part I've played in the sinister reality they've been building for years. I feel like a soldier who returns from war to learn he'd killed children over a fight for oil, orchestrated by a machine bigger than him. I joined NXIVM to be part of a positive movement in the world, to do good.

Am I bad?

What have I done?

THE WOMEN

2009

"If every city had a leader like Sarah, this company would be unstoppable."

NXIVM president Nancy Salzman was known to deliver this line to our coaching team and while speaking in front of hundreds of NXIVM students. When she started praising me like this, it was 2009, and the company was booming. Across our four branches in Mexico, Los Angeles, Albany, and the Canadian headquarters I'd recently co-founded in my native Vancouver, we were enlisting hundreds of new members every month. We'd just enrolled one of the world's most beloved actresses in one of our coaching programs; a famous Hollywood actor was hosting one of our retreats at his mansion in Los Feliz; *and* I had recently performed a one-on-one coaching session for an iconic legend of rock 'n' roll, whose life choices had been landing him in the gossip columns for decades. I'd led him through our process known as an EM (exploration of meaning), and I observed quietly while he suddenly recalled a memory from deep in his past. His gaze, which had initially seemed so worn and exhausted, widened into instant enlightenment. I allowed him a minute to realize that the event he was remembering had led to years of a behavior pattern that had been unhealthy for him. I broke the silence by asking, "What do you make it mean?" This was a routine benchmark for every EM. I was trained to facilitate shifts like this one every day . . . but for him? In that moment, we both knew that his life had just changed.

There's no question we were having an impact. The executives told us that a workshop had just been held on Necker Island, a private resort in the Caribbean owned by Richard Branson. We were making such a difference in the world that the Dalai Lama spoke at a NXIVM event and even agreed to provide the foreword for the book that our founder, Keith Raniere, had written. Some of the best-known CEOs, actors, and spiritual figures on the planet had endorsed him—and *we* were his megaphone, his tentacles that reached out into the world and drew new followers ever more curious to discover him. I grew up believing that every person has the power to make a change in the world. As part of this company, and now with our Vancouver center growing faster than I could ever have hoped, I was living that dream.

The progress was profound not only because of what I was part of, but because of how far I personally had come. Just four years before, I'd been a lost young actress searching for everything: my big break, a way to save some money, friends I could connect with, and—more than anything—my purpose in life.

And I believed I had found it, as a salesperson for one of the most groundbreaking companies in the world, where I held the highest enrollment closing rate in the organization. I didn't just persuade new recruits that NXIVM's principles worked; I was proof they did because they'd worked in my own life. I wholeheartedly believed in them. NXIVM was making great strides in evolving consciousness among individuals and promoting world peace.

Nancy Salzman's praise fell on me like I was a rescued puppy waiting for crumbs. Known to ESP students as Prefect, Nancy had been Keith Raniere's right hand since they founded NXIVM in 1998. She wasn't only the self-help group's highest coach; she was the head of the school, there to motivate the staff (her "pseudo-children," as she called us) and develop new content to sell. The organization was known, both internally and to people outside of it, as a community, a corporation, and a way of life.

At the start, Keith had asked a mutual friend to approach Nancy, who we were told was a renowned therapist and who supposedly had worked as a consultant for organizations like Con Edison, New York City's power authority; American Express; and the State of New

York itself. Keith offered Nancy what some therapists might dream of having: an opportunity to shape a personal development curriculum that would totally disrupt all existing psychotherapeutic modalities and self-help systems. In return, Nancy pledged her career to Keith and used her training to create lesson plans that would lead to break-throughs in people's understanding of themselves. As the program grew, the two of them built its marketing on what they said was the foundation of Nancy's career. It was touted that she'd worked as a therapist before she moved into coaching leaders toward their poten-tial, and she had studied with some masters who had contributed to the field of psychology. Nancy's own specialty was neurolinguistic programming (NLP), a technique for understanding how the brain processes words, which she'd learned from NLP's two founders, Richard Bandler and John Grinder. She told us that NLP was consid-ered to be more effective at changing an individual's behavior than years of therapy or even hypnosis, which she had also mastered after studying Milton Erickson's unconventional approach to psychother-apy. Nancy had an over-the-top, zany way of presenting material and was known to go into hysterics at her own jokes, but when it came to growth—personal or within the NXIVM corporation—I didn't dare question her.

Unfortunately, not even her mastery of these paradigms would be enough to save her from the fate she'd encounter as the president of Keith Raniere's organization.

Away from an audience, Nancy could be harshly critical—but over the years she'd pushed me, and she had my respect. I'd earned a degree in theater and cut my teeth as an actress. I could bear tough cri-tiques, and I was no stranger to hustle. Her recommendations worked; and as I grew my skill in sales and added to the company's profit, she lavished me in compliments and dangled the carrot of financial incentives. "We're starting a new curriculum track," she'd say, "and *you* could make a *ton* of money." The money hadn't been my original moti-vation to work for them—the personal growth, sense of purpose, and community had been—but by now, there was no higher compliment for me than when Nancy praised my sales performance and welcomed me into NXIVM's inner circle of senior-level executives. This team of five women, plus a handful of others, was a growing force.

Barbara Bouchey was an important mentor in my early days. A financial planner who joined Keith and Nancy in 1999, right after they started NXIVM, Barbara said she found the material helpful in overcoming the pain of her divorce. After Keith and Nancy had acquainted her with their new program, she jumped on board to help them grow the company. She had untamed blond hair and was one of the first to coach me in recruiting people to enroll in the Executive Success Program. Barbara was strong willed; intelligent if a bit eccentric, a figure I grew closer with as she went out of her way to show me the ropes. When I first joined and was still earning my way to climb up the system of promotion the company called "the Stripe Path," Barbara used her airline points to fly me from Vancouver to Albany so that I could attend an important corporate event. She believed in me from the beginning and was one of the first to invest in my potential.

Pam Cafritz had been Keith's longtime indispensable assistant for almost thirty years and was one of the company's only two purple sashes on the Stripe Path. She had come from a socialite family in Washington, D.C., and was on a ski trip when she first met Keith. They were both in their twenties. He often told the story of how he had pushed his way through the line to take the chairlift with her. As they exited toward the slope, he told her, "Follow me." And she did. Often at the center of the whirlwind around Keith, Pam reminded me of a doe in the woods—lean and quiet, always thoughtfully tuned in to the activity around her. When it came to my growth in the organization, Pam was happy to sit down and "work me through my issues" if I needed extra help. She often suggested I should spend more time with Keith as part of my commitment to grow in the organization . . . though, to be honest, I often found myself keeping a little distance from them both.

Barb Jeske, lovingly known as "Barb J.," held the only other purple sash. We called her Madame Reality because she was so frank and smart—by far my favorite coach. Her candid personality and angular features were offset by a certain softness in her nature. She was the zero-makeup type and had flaxen hair that fell past her waist. It was always as though there were two sides to her. She was no-nonsense but almost maternal. Everything about her came from a place of concern for us as her staff and her devotion to the material we taught and practiced. Barb J. and I shared a similar passion for healthy living—kombucha, coconut water, and green juice. Over the years, we spent many long walks together discussing how to be the healthiest and best version of ourselves.

And there was my best friend, Lauren. Lauren was the driven, heart-centered companion I'd longed for since I was a kid—as well as the daughter of my boss, Nancy Salzman. Lauren was the person who had changed my life from the moment I met her. In 2005 when I attended my very first introductory NXIVM seminar, known to us as "the Five-Day," I'd found myself zoning out from the DVDs they played for us. The turning point arrived when, in one of the videos, I heard Nancy Salzman mention her daughter, Lauren, who she said was also part of NXIVM's corporation. Nancy explained that Lauren had always been the type of person who would quit any activity that didn't come easily to her. *That's me*, I thought. *I never push through anything.* I'd often given up if something wasn't panning out quickly or I wasn't catching on right away . . . and on some level I knew this had been part of the reason I was still searching for my direction in life. In the video, Nancy explained that if I were *truly* committed to my personal growth, this organization would arm me with a community of peers and coaches who would support me as I worked my way up the NXIVM ladder, the Stripe Path, likening it to "the martial arts system of personal growth." That definitely appealed to me, as I'd struggled to stay on target in my acting career. You could go into auditions appearing attractive and performing well—you could be everything a role called for—and often you still wouldn't get the part. I liked the idea of a consistent standard I could be measured against. The Stripe Path offered that.

That had been four years earlier. By 2009, these women—all high-achieving, free-thinking, and financially independent—had become the people who were closer to me than anyone. Others had also joined the ranks in Albany, some of whom I'd enrolled: Nicki Clyne, an acting colleague I'd invited from Vancouver, along with Allison Mack, who came to her first Jness intensive at the suggestion of a friend in Vancouver. There were the ones who'd moved to Albany from Mexico because, I believed, they'd been lured by the chance to advance in the company or wanted to be part of the community.

Our job as coaches in this program was to transform thinking in the world, and Nancy's job was to make sure we were reaching an ever-growing community. Personally and professionally, I was inspired, and there's no question that I'd grown past so many of my old limitations. It was these women, and a handful of others, who had made me part of this mission.

I'd demonstrated my potential and earned a place, albeit still pretty early on the Stripe Path, among this legion of women—all NXIVM executives—who had all found ways to take me under their wing to urge my growth. We were our own subcommunity of NXIVM, building our own little culture while helping the larger organization crush it on a global level.

But for the twelve years I was in NXIVM, I had no clue that every single one of these women was keeping an important secret. Every time all of us gathered into one space for a training, a sales meeting, or to brainstorm new curricula, I had no idea there was such a strong likelihood that each of them had at some point been Keith Raniere's sexual partner. In fact, as these women worked closely with one another over the years to develop new education, sales, and enrollment strategies, every single one of them thought that Keith had chosen her as his one-and-only lifelong soulmate while he thought of them *all*, collectively, as his "spiritual wives."

None of us knew that his teachings, which promised to make us leaders, were actually making us followers—*his* followers. His disciples. He wanted us to worship him. None of us knew how Keith's machinations and manipulations would come to impact our lives; that we weren't learning from him as much as we were being indoctrinated and deceived—brainwashed—by him. I would come to learn that while purporting to bond us closer as strong, evolved women, Keith was undermining our relationships to each other in a harrowing, behind-the-scenes way and trying to eliminate the relationship each of us had with ourselves—for his own personal benefit. A self-proclaimed science, literature, and history buff, Keith chose the very name NXIVM when he created the company in 1998 as a reference to a debt bondage system in the time of Julius Caesar. We had been told that NXIVM meant "a place of learning," but after I got out and started doing some research, I learned that in ancient times, a "nexum" was a person pledging his or her services as collateral for the repayment of a debt, and the person owed the debt (the "master") was allowed to demand services indefinitely. This included sexual services. Keith loved masterminding terms like this, with a reference to something illicit that only he would understand.

We didn't know that Keith had created a dangerous psychological hierarchy among us. That he didn't think of us as the principal leaders of his company—that instead, he thought of us as the most devout followers in his cult and that, as he told Barbara Bouchey in a conversation she videotaped in 2009, "I've had people killed for my beliefs." During the era that I thought was our prime, a few of the women were just beginning to discover that their involvement with NXIVM had not been a path toward their purpose but the worst mistake of their lives.

In 2009, I was at the top of my game, fulfilled by my work financially and emotionally. I was surrounded by an intergenerational group of women who were mentors, mother figures, and best friends. I thought I was living the dream, making my living by spreading goodness and enlightenment in the world. I believed we were the luckiest—and most revolutionary—women on the planet.

What I didn't know was that my commitment to these women and this organization would indeed cause my life to transform and force me to grow stronger, but it wouldn't be with them at my side. Over the next eight years, some of my close friends would vanish, two of my coaches would lose their lives, and my blind following of this community would eventually be vanquished by my intuition—all shortly after my best friend, Lauren, lured me into her home and instructed me to get naked.

PART ONE

ETHICAL VALUE EXCHANGE

2005–2009

CHAPTER ONE

BASE ASSUMPTION

2005
THE BAHAMAS

Throughout my childhood I often felt conflicted between wanting to fit in and expressing my own voice. Raised in Vancouver by two endearing mental health professionals who were influenced by the social climate and political activism of the 1960s and early '70s when they met, one of my strongest childhood memories is of the time I took a My Little Pony toy from one of the girls in my Brownie troop when I was eight. That night at home, with compassion and without judgment, my mother sat down on my bed and led me in a reflective conversation on why what I had done was not OK and how I needed to repair it. She shared with me that she believed a child will sometimes steal when he or she feels like something has been taken away from them. Mom was like the Jewish-Canadian Joan Baez—highly intelligent, flowing hair, floor-length velvet dresses, Moroccan beads, and folk music. With her academic concentration in early childhood education, she raised me in a way that honored her belief that children should be nurtured with respect, and space to develop and discover who they are.

Goodness was a value my parents shared. My mom fell in love with my father after university in the 1970s, when they worked with a group of friends to open a vegetarian café in Yorkshire, England, called Alligator (which I recently learned still exists). My dad has always been the type of individual who didn't waver from his beliefs, even when it cost him. As a young man, he renounced the British aristocratic tradition of his parents, an actual lord and lady, and instead chose to march on the docks for fair pay and better working conditions for union workers. The way I think of my dad from when I was a kid is remembering how he'd sing with his guitar as he marched in peaceful protests.

Even after they split when I was almost three, my parents joined in the most progressive, conscious way to raise me as partners before "co-parenting" was a thing. They enrolled me in kindergarten in a neighborhood school that felt like its own little island; a brick schoolhouse on a sprawling field overlooking the series of beaches known as the Spanish Banks. I lived for classes like literature and theater. With an active imagination, I often played pretend by myself, especially because I was one of only two girls in my kindergarten class. After school, while the athletic boys played soccer, I engaged in make-believe with the gentle-natured boys in my class or walked a block home to make jewelry and hair wraps that I sold down on the beach in the summer.

Each summer from the age of twelve, my parents sent me off to an extreme left-wing Jewish summer camp, from where I'd return with the confidence to tell the high school boys to fuck off when they held up their hands and yelled, "Heil, Hitler!" I loved my summers away at camp because this was where I first felt such a strong sense of belonging and where as a teen I developed my leadership skills as a camp counselor. Back in school, I found my social circle among the drama kids and went to high school in striped tights and Doc Martens, or decked out in purple from my shirt to my bell bottoms, all the way down to my Converse. My body didn't gain curves until my senior year of high school, which only added to the teasing and my self-consciousness. It hadn't been cool to be a Jewish theater geek in Vancouver . . . and it certainly hadn't been cool to be *this* Jewish theater geek. Cute? Perhaps. Lovable? If big purple glasses and braces were your thing, then sure. But even in the presence of my friends, I often felt like an outsider.

In high school when most teenagers were sneaking off to drink and make out, I attended my first personal development workshop at a retreat center that my mom recommended that was off the coast and only accessible by ferry. Engrained with my parents' interests in psychology and what makes people tick, I had started my introspective journey. Eventually, I found myself in the theater scene in our high school, where I made a group of friends I could relate to and hang out with. Acting became the place where I could express myself and feel like I belonged, both onstage and off.

Meanwhile, my parents had always taught me the importance of making the world a better place. In all of my challenges as a dorky teen, I didn't understand that my differences would later be the driving force to help me make an impact. I thought pursuing a career in acting could give me that platform. I graduated from university in Montreal with a BFA in theater in 2000. After choosing between psychology and acting, I had landed some great leading TV roles while I was at university, but after three years there, I missed the lifestyle in Vancouver. I'd grown up loving hikes in the forest and mountains, walks on the beach, my favorite yoga studios, health food restaurants, and the cafés with smoothies and fresh pressed juices. And most of all, I missed my family. My mom had been experiencing some health problems, and I figured I could move back to Vancouver and support her during this time. A lot of studios in Los Angeles had begun to migrate to Vancouver to shoot their productions more cheaply, so I could look for an agent to start getting auditions. For some income I took a waitressing job that gave me days off to try out for parts, but after work I found myself reuniting with old friends who'd grown well acquainted with the Vancouver party scene in the time I'd been studying out east. We had some fun and very late nights, and before I knew it, those few months at my mom's house turned into three years.

I knew that pot and parties weren't the path to getting on my feet. Here and there I would land bit parts on TV shows that would bring in enough money to string me along, but the trend was toward shows inspired by nineties supernatural series like *Buffy the Vampire Slayer*. Beer commercials and knockoff vampire shows weren't really the beginnings of a promising career. Plus, due to the Hollywood writers' strike in 2001, production in general dwindled and auditions were slim.

In 2002, I met a really sweet guy through friends. David was an aspiring filmmaker who was also trying to get his start, and ours became my first serious relationship as an adult. We quickly moved in together and lived in the young couple's proverbial basement apartment a few blocks from the beach on Vancouver's trendy West Side. We were always brainstorming ideas for film projects and had similar crowds of friends, but after a couple of years, I was growing restless. Our apartment was dark and cramped, and our careers felt just as limited. A few of the books I'd read had suggested that to move closer to our goals, we had to surround ourselves with people who had what we wanted. That was it: I told David we needed to plug ourselves into some kind of powerful network, a group of creative professionals who would support each other's success. I called some fellow actors and formed a circle to work our way through Julia Cameron's *The Artist's Way* in a support-group setting. It was a start, I felt, but most of us were still struggling to land meaningful work.

Around this time, David learned that one of his short films had been accepted into the Spiritual Cinema Circle Festival at Sea. As the festival's guests, we could attend for free as long as we could cover the cost of the weeklong Caribbean cruise. David and I knew it would be a stretch, but as we read about the festival on its website, we agreed it could be worth it. I, for one, had been starving for purpose and fulfillment, and being part of this kind of setting was what I needed to stay motivated. David was equally enthusiastic, honored that his film had been chosen for a screening by filmmakers he admired.

The festival was celebrating filmmakers who were creating works with social impact and that aimed to raise consciousness. It was endorsed by Deepak Chopra and led by Stephen Simon, who made the spiritual Hollywood hit *What Dreams May Come,* starring Robin Williams. This would be a chance to meet some influencers in our industry. We were also really excited because the director of *What the Bleep Do We Know!?*—at the time a very popular new age documentary on spirituality and quantum physics—was going to be the judge of the films and the guest of honor.

I had been reading a lot of self-help and spirituality books like *The Celestine Prophecy* and by authors like Eckhart Tolle. Works like these about the quest for purpose inspired me to seek out spiritually like-minded people. When I heard about the cruise, I sensed there would be great networking opportunities, and as I had been learning about "manifesting," before we boarded the ship I set an intention to meet people who were living their purpose so I could gain some direction in finding mine. Little did I know we would share a dinner table at sea with the man whose friendship would alter the course of my life.

It all started with a chest cold. Before we boarded the ship, I hadn't been able to get over a horrible seal-bark cough I'd been fighting for days. Now that we were on board and attending theater screenings on the ship, others on the cruise had been turning to look at me. At the kickoff dinner on the first night, one of the other guests at our table leaned in toward me. "What would you lose if you were to stop coughing?" he whispered.

Huh? I was startled by his candidness, until I detected a twinkle in his eye. In a uniquely caring way, he was really inviting me to contemplate this.

I sat there, scanning old memories. I remembered when feeling sick meant that my normally very active parents would put their lives on hold to take care of me. Wait—could there have been an association between being sick and getting attention? It occurred to me that David's career had recently taken center stage in our relationship, and I'd begun to feel like I had to work for him to notice me.

In this instant, the connection between the two phenomena clicked into place. I laughed, trying to appear that I could brush his observation off with charm . . . but as he smiled and looked back toward the evening's onstage presentation, I took a sip of my water while willing myself to gain control of my cough, and my emotion about this realization. *Who is he?* I thought, eyeing his profile while he listened to the dinner's emcee. He was young but distinguished, with glasses and a very assured expression. His insight was powerful.

Over dinner, I learned exactly who this was: Mark Vicente, the film director my boyfriend and I had been so hopeful for the chance to meet. Right away, I liked and respected Mark. He seemed a little standoffish at first, but as he warmed up over dinner, he was generous with his wisdom about our industry and how to put meaningful thought out into the world. Just like the book I'd read had argued, all

I'd needed to do was set the intention to begin to meet the kind of people who would help me find my purpose. Could it be so simple? It was already working!

By the next day, my cough had faded, and David and I had clicked with Mark. Together we all spent the week at sea watching films in the ship's theater and exploring the tropics while in port. One morning while wading knee-deep in crystal waters, Mark shared with us that he'd recently joined an organization run by Keith Raniere, whom he said was one of the smartest men in the world. He explained that about five years earlier, Keith had started NXIVM (pronounced "NEX-ee-um"), a community of humanitarians who were spending their time and resources to shift the state of humanity. Mark explained that NXIVM had lined up with his purpose so much that he'd begun working with them, and he was learning their methodology to have his filmmaking be more impactful.

The chance to do good combined with the chance to work with Mark? I tried not to squeeze David's arm in hopes he'd be on board with doing this. This sounded exactly like what I'd been looking for.

Mark also said it just so happened that a month later, NXIVM was holding its first-ever Canadian intensive. Out of all the cities across all of Canada, it was meant to be: this workshop, known to introductory students as the Five-Day, would be held in Vancouver. Mark said instructors from different branches like New York would be flying in to lead us in NXIVM's powerful five-day process for taking steps toward our dreams.

Like producing films with you? I thought. "Where do I sign up?" I asked him.

Mark enrolled me while we were still on the cruise and introduced David and me to a woman named Suzanne who was also onboard and involved with NXIVM. "Are you interested in learning more about the community?" she asked.

"Yeah," I said. "I'm super into it."

When I saw Suzanne again later that day, she approached me with an application. "The down payment for the first level-one intensive is $500," she said.

Hold on, I thought. *This* sounds *like a good investment, but I could really use a little more time to give it thought.* I told Suzanne we needed to think about this. As David and I talked it over later that day, the notion flashed through my mind that if we didn't sign up, Mark would perceive us as wishy-washy. That was *not* how I wanted us to come across to a guy who not only had so much sway in our industry, but who was literally holding out his playbook for success for us to accept. *It's an investment in myself,* I thought. *It's not like I'm committing my life.* Still, five hundred dollars was more than my share of a month's rent for our apartment.

For the next two days it seemed like Suzanne would turn up wherever I was around the ship. "People who don't commit to their growth in the beginning end up never committing to it at all," she persisted. I became so weirded out by her that I started to feel I'd be willing to pay that money just so she'd stop following me around. "Should we just do it?" I asked David.

"If you sign up within forty-eight hours of hearing about the course, you'll get a discount on the total cost," Suzanne said. David rubbed his hair, trying to force a hurried decision. "I guess so," he said.

Now relaxed and smiling, Suzanne took my application. Then she held out her hand while David looked at me before handing his application over too. "This five hundred is actually a bargain for both of you," she said.

"Really?" I asked. "How?"

"Total cost?" David asked. "How much is that?"

"It's $2,160 U.S. dollars. Normally, it's $2700."

He and I looked at each other in a panic. That was about $2,500 Canadian, each. That was a serious chunk of money.

Back home outside the bubble of Mark Vicente's idealism, David and I agreed we had to come to our senses: $2,160 U.S. dollars?! I freaked out about the financial commitment. I phoned NXIVM's headquarters in Albany, New York. "I don't have the money," I pleaded with the woman on the phone. "I'd like to get my deposit back."

She was just as pushy as Suzanne had been. "You're twenty-eight years old and you don't have any money? How will that ever change if you don't address your beliefs around finances?"

Touché. I understood she had a point. "But," I said, "I'm an actress, and if I'm inside a seminar for five days and my agent calls, I won't be available for auditions."

Without missing a beat, she laid it on me: "Would you like to wait around for your agent to call you, or be the master of your own ship?"

Checkmate. Of course I wanted to be the master of my own ship. (I also wanted this woman to stop being so blunt with me.) I put the remaining $1,660 American on my credit card.

It's just money. Maybe that woman was right. Maybe this $2,000 will be a good investment. What was that saying? You have to spend money to make money?

At the time, I told myself it wasn't a big deal, and I tried to tell David the same. However, our first sign that something was amiss was the feeling that we were being cornered into committing. This kind of tactic isn't recruitment as much as it is coercion. I should have also listened to the feeling inside me when Suzanne was so insistent on getting our money.

Later I'd also learn that lines like "most people never commit" were language used to promote NXIVM's system of superiority over others. The attitude that one person is more informed/enlightened/ powerful than another was a trademark of the company I'd grow more familiar with over time.

This down payment was the beginning of what I would invest into NXIVM for the next decade-plus to come. It all started with preying on my money. Then they would work to take my mind, my heart—

And eventually, my body.

INTEGRATION

SUMMER 2005
VANCOUVER

When David and I signed up for our first Five-Day training, I was expecting to walk into an arena full of hundreds of people, like a Tony Robbins conference. Instead, we made our way into a dingy conference room inside a Holiday Inn Express in Burnaby, British Columbia, twenty minutes east of Vancouver. We cautiously took our seats in a semicircle of beat-up chairs with nine other attendees and a continental breakfast from Bread Garden—Canada's version of Panera. I smiled at a couple of the other introductory students, wondering what professions allowed them to take five days away from their work, too.

The first morning of that seminar, this was one of several questions I had. I also had to wonder: why were the leaders instructing us to refer to NXIVM's founder, Keith Raniere, by the name Vanguard? Why were we paying what they called "tribute" to him, like prayers recited as a group, when he wasn't even in the room? And why did I just pay over $2,000 to watch a video? The video starred Nancy Salzman, the company's president, who addressed the camera in a shoulder-padded suit and scholarly spectacles while seeming never to pause for a breath. I struggled to stay fully alert, while via video she walked us through emotional processes and drew diagrams like a too-serious game of Pictionary while she declared that she'd never seen anything like the tools she'd gained through ESP. *Blah blah blah*, I thought. What was her deal? I couldn't quite look past her

1990s Murphy Brown style or the way she gushed about NXIVM's Executive Success Program in every video that the facilitators of the intensive inserted into the DVD player. Nancy's presentation was campy and overdone. "You have to meet Nancy Salzman in person," Mark Vicente had assured me on the cruise, in what now seemed to preempt any doubt I might have felt compelled to express. *Fair enough*, I thought. Mark had said Keith was the smartest man in the world. If Mark saw a legitimate reason to endorse her, then I'd give Nancy a chance.

In the first module, called Rules & Rituals, I found that I was constantly talking myself into overlooking the inescapable weirdness of the organization. On video Nancy introduced the NXIVM handshake, where instead of two hands meeting on the same lateral plane, the person who was higher on the Stripe Path positioned their palm on top of the palm of the lower-level student whose hand they were shaking. Nancy explained that the point of the Five-Day was to create an ethical framework of understanding by establishing a working definition for basic concepts, like good and bad, right and wrong, honesty and disclosure. This would make our belief systems ethical and consistent. In the video, she explained that as we moved through the material, we might find ourselves feeling something that she referred to as "the urge to bolt," and if we do, that's just our internal indication that we were doing it right. Discomfort was an indication you were "hitting on an issue," so if you bolted, you would never work that limiting belief. Then she reviewed some of the community's common terms, which to me sounded like overly cerebral, scientific words, in the same way you'd develop a secret code language with your best friend in grade school. Their word *data* was just "information," *class-one* could be translated to firsthand ("You heard that rumor but didn't receive that as class-one data"). A *viscera* was our body's reaction to stimuli in temperature, movement, and pressure, usually in our guts as a fight or flight response. We might say something like, "When I opened my bank statement, I freaked out! I had such a bad viscera." Mark was right. The material on the first two days felt a little hard to digest. I felt very resistant, sitting back with my arms folded as if to say, *What can you possibly teach me? My parents were therapists.* I overheard one of the coaches behind me say that NXIVM's word for resistant was "defiant," so I uncrossed my arms and straightened myself out of my slouched position.

Before we had started the Five-Day, we signed a form promising we'd keep the text, materials, and curriculum private, and together we recited NXIVM's twelve-point mission statement. In it, we declared ideas such as that we are all interdependent; that for each of us to be successful would contribute to the development of "a better world; a world free from hunger, theft, dishonesty, envy, and insecurity"; that under any circumstance, we would choose never to be a victim.

Then the leaders who were facilitating the Five-Day introduced themselves as coming from the Tacoma ESP (Executive Success Program) center. They distributed booklets printed on card stock in shades of blue and red that reminded me of a sweater my grandfather in England had worn when I was a kid. The font looked like it had come from the 1970s, and the cover read: *Throughout the ages there have always been men and women who have broken barriers, exceeded expectations, and established new norms. All had one thing in common. The ancient Greeks called it "Ethos" (the driving spirit).*

Ethos was the name of an ongoing program within ESP, which centered on the idea that true success stemmed from a rare emotional strength. As they painted it, it was simple: lots of people want to be successful, but few actually are. Why haven't you achieved greater success? the pamphlet asked. It suggested it was because success is an "emotionally based activity."

The wording felt awkward to me—success wasn't an activity. Success is an idea.

The pamphlet called other success principles "useless" and promoted the Ethos program as something that could help one "make the leap from knowing about success . . . to actually having success." And then they hit you: "We are an ongoing program that helps you develop the necessary inner strengths to achieve success. It's a team effort with team support."

Ongoing? Team support? That I liked.

"Plus, you have a personal coach to guide you and provide the encouragement you need to realize your full potential."

Here, it's important to remember that all this was before *Eat Pray Love*. We were still a few years ahead of the time when thousands of people would leave the corporate jobs they found devoid of soul and either *hired* a "life coach" or *became* a "life coach." The concept of having someone who would hold me accountable to my goals and impart wisdom and transformational practices was a big sell, even if there were other parts of the ESP pitch that didn't quite resonate.

The cover of the pamphlet featured the images of figures like Martin Luther King Jr. and Albert Einstein—people I knew hadn't achieved their success through NXIVM. *OK*, I thought, *don't be judgy, Sarah*. As I paged through the pamphlet, I found blocks of text with headings like "An Extraordinary Resource That Can Change Your Life!" and the word *Ethos*, always accompanied by the trademark symbol in superscript; the worksheets they handed out read: *Copyright 1999, Executive Success Programs, Inc. All rights reserved. Patent Pending. Confidential. Not for publication or distribution.*

Impressive, I thought. *So they've actually trademarked these concepts.*

That veil of legitimacy overshadowed my gut feeling that the follow-through was lacking or that their claims were lofty.

I spent the first day waiting for the good stuff. David and I had come here for the sky's-the-limit career inspiration and the exercises to evolve our consciousness in ways that would change the world. Instead, I found that the material wasn't a ton of fun to sit through. On the first couple of days of the Five-Day, I continued to page through this pamphlet, finding images of Abraham Lincoln, Colonel Sanders, Amelia Earhart, Marie Curie. Muriel Siebert, who according to the caption next to her photo was "the first woman member of NY Stock Exchange. Has thirteen honorary doctoral degrees and never finished college."

OK, but . . . what did they have to do with NXIVM's ESP? Clearly all these individuals had achieved noteworthy things, but what was the connection? "Take Edmund Hillary," the text said, "a mere beekeeper who in 1952 attempted to summit Mount Everest. . . . During a lecture a few weeks after his failed attempt, Edmund Hillary showed the mountain had not diminished his inner resolve. He made a fist and pointed to a picture of the mountain and said with fierce determination, 'Mount Everest, you beat me the first time, but I'll beat you the next time.'"

Who wrote this stuff?

The vibe was off for me—like this should be on a coffee table in a 1980s corporate building lobby. But if they took themselves this seriously, could it be because they were truly onto discoveries that we all want for ourselves?

This was consistent with the experience I had with everything in NXIVM: there was some messaging that sounded like total bullshit, while some material held real insight quality. On the afternoon of the first day of the Five-Day, Nancy explained in the video that following the Stripe Path means to earn various levels of colored sashes by taking courses, bringing in new members, and focusing on eliminating our own limitations. I began to think of this as my chance to commit to my personal growth in a way I'd be held accountable to.

The Stripe Path was laid out so that each new stripe or sash was earned on the basis of three criteria:

- your skill level with the "tech" (how many courses you'd taken)

- how many people you'd enrolled

- and how many "integrations" you'd experienced, thanks to your dedication to working out old, unsuccessful emotional patterns from your past.

The progression of these colored sashes on the Stripe Path went from:

- white (student)

- yellow (coach)

- orange (proctor)

- green (senior proctor)

- blue (counselor, which only one individual in the company's history had reached)
- purple (senior counselor, only Barb Jeske and Pam Cafritz had ever reached the status of a purple sash)

Nancy Salzman held the organization's only gold sash. As we continued deeper into the Five-Day, I also heard that the difference between the use of the word NXIVM versus the term ESP was that NXIVM was the actual company, while ESP referred to the program within the company that taught personal development intensives.

Nancy explained that the people in the higher ranks, under Keith, had reached their respective levels of success by truly living the foundational philosophy of ESP: "being at-cause." This concept was defined as the understanding that we, as individuals, cause everything that happens to us. Whether it's money, success, romance, or anything else we seek, ESP would deliver a perceptual shift that we are "causing agents" in our lives. "Being at-cause is taking responsibility for your participation in the laws of cause and effect," Nancy said. She revealed that being at-cause allows one to make better decisions and to own all of his or her choices.

To be "at-cause" also meant that we choose our emotions. This caught my attention when Nancy explained how we know this to be true: because no two people respond to the same stimulus in the same way. The example that Nancy used was that if a man walks in on his wife with another man, he could choose to respond in a number of different ways. He could be so angry that he runs to get his gun. He might act as a voyeur and get a camera. Or he could be happy because he wanted a divorce and now has a justification. There isn't one automatic response or reaction we all exhibit when something significant transpires in our lives.

Being at-cause is a way of life, Nancy said. Living this way means you recognize that you are the cause of everything in your life. For someone to behave "out of cause" means that they're choosing to be a victim instead of recognizing their "at-causedness," or *how* their role in the situation caused what happened.

"All successful people can see how effective this material is right away," Nancy stated. Here, I started to pay more attention. Then, she invited us to do an exercise determining our "values hierarchy," writing down the aspects of our life that were most important to us.

Numbers one and two came easily:

1. CREATIVITY AND EXPRESSION (ACTING)

2. PERSONAL GROWTH

The rest of my list took a little more thought, but the point of the exercise was that it provided a breakthrough, as Nancy noted, to prioritize your values and rank them in order one by one. She taught us that many people can't make decisions because they aren't clear on what their priorities are, as they haven't been able to figure out which values are more important than others, causing a "values conflict." This resonated deeply for me. I was always having trouble making decisions, so this ranked list would be so helpful. But over time, I would eventually swap my numbers one and two. Through pressure to attend ESP trainings over family events, such as my grandfather's birthday, I received tacit suggestions that personal growth needed to be my highest value if I was going to advance in NXIVM. The Stripe Path had to trump all other values. Including family.

The content grew increasingly analytical and centered on understanding our own psychology, which was a lot more interesting. On day three, we started to examine self-esteem. ESP taught it as more than simply the middle-school guidance counselor definition of the way we feel about ourselves. We learned that self-esteem can also be seen as our "options" in a given area.

We were asked to list areas in our lives in which we didn't feel good about ourselves. I wrote: my career. In the breakout group, the coaches helped me brainstorm options to help me in this area: take an acting class, find a mentor, read biographies of great actresses. By listing out some options, I felt more optimistic, and I also started to apply this exercise to other areas of my life. This new definition of self-esteem totally rocked my world.

Nancy also walked us through an analysis of how we each choose to define the word "good." I hadn't ever realized before that we take this idea for granted. She introduced a system of sussing out what's good from what's bad by first arriving at an objective definition of value, which is anything that saves time and effort. Good builds value, and bad destroys value. Using this definition, what's good versus what's bad can be measured objectively from one individual to the next. The curriculum also explained that it would address many issues in the world if we could all agree upon what's good versus what's bad.

Rational Inquiry, Prefect taught, is a way for an individual to explore their inner workings, either on their own or with the support of a coach, to figure out where the inconsistencies in their beliefs lie. It's inconsistent to think of money as the root of all evil when you also want it. Or if one parent instructs a child, "Always tell the truth," but the other parent says, "You shouldn't hurt anyone's feelings," these may be counter-commands. When a friend steps out of the fitting room in something you don't find flattering and asks you, "I really like this dress, what do you think?" if you lie, you may experience a physical reaction, known as—*I got it!*—a viscera.

As that Five-Day seminar progressed with thirteen hours of lessons per day, I found that I had two big emotional breakthroughs when I engaged in my first in-depth emotional NXIVM process, which was known as EM (exploration of meaning). This was an exercise we did to examine a stimulus that had long triggered a negative emotional reaction in us, in what they called a stimulus/response pattern. In my case, my first EM exercise helped me to soothe an ongoing gripe between David and myself when I "integrated" the reason I got so upset when he left unwashed dishes in the sink was because of an early childhood belief that dishes had actually caused my parents' divorce. My earliest memory was of witnessing my parents fight over that issue right before they separated, and in my mind, dirty dishes had become linked with the worst time of my early life. When NXIVM's tools helped me to observe the association that I'd created, I was able to "unhook" it so that it wouldn't have such a detrimental impact anymore.

I'd been having a similar experience with a stimulus-response pattern around David not coming to bed at the same time as I did, which to me made me feel like he didn't love me. In my childhood, I linked love with bedtime, as that was when I felt most loved by and connected to my parents while they sang to me, tickled my back, or read me bedtime stories. I'd made a leap in my logic to believe that if you love someone, heading to bed at the same time was just what you do. So now, if my boyfriend was not there with me when I went to sleep, I felt like he didn't love me.

The whole premise of ESP was that our belief systems, or "operating systems," were formed before we had full adult logic—so naturally there were flaws in the cause-and-effect events we experienced in the world. We were told that if we formed that blueprint at a time when we still believed in Santa Claus, then of course we would hold other beliefs that weren't based in reality. As part of Keith Raniere's science-inspired "technology," Nancy claimed that ESP would "upgrade your programming."

These seemingly simple breakthroughs—such as that dishes or going to sleep at the same time as your partner did not make or break a relationship—were my first integrations. In ESP, this happens when your belief system finally aligns to reality. The people from the Tacoma center taught us that, with other therapeutic methods, people learned to replace their responses with another response or behavior, such as an alcoholic who transferred the need for alcohol to attending AA meetings; or someone who's afraid of speaking in public and takes Xanax to deal with that fear. These inferior methods were simply Band-Aids, Keith said, and ESP was the only thing that removed a stimulus-response permanently, and in a short period of time. Nancy and the upper ranks insisted that most people go to therapy for years to accomplish what we were doing.

In my case, ESP was instantly helpful. The power of NXIVM's curriculum, which Nancy called the "tech," made it easier for me to look past the chintziness of the presentation. I wondered: if that EM, that exploration of meaning, could bring peace to one small issue in my life, could it work for more than that? I was curious and hopeful enough to keep a somewhat open mind.

On day one of that seminar, they gave each of us a white sash, which they explained was a "student sash"—a long piece of fabric they instructed us to wear around our necks so that it fell to mid-torso on both sides. They'd told us that the Stripe Path measured one's "growth" or "level of integration." I looked down at my sash. I didn't like it; I thought the idea (and the fabric) was cheap and embarrassing, and I didn't like that they were taking it upon themselves to measure us as people when they didn't even know us. I didn't appreciate being considered at the bottom of the ranks, nor did I like the ranking system. Meanwhile, David was having a meltdown, relating these ranks to the corrupt regime in the country he'd been born in, which he and his family had emigrated from when he was a preteen. Neither of us was fully on board with this. "Should we leave?" I asked him. He gave me a look that seemed to say, *Sarah, we spent so much money to be here.* When we got home that night, we talked more about our reservations and got out our laptops to research a bit more. A *Forbes* article came up about Keith with the title "Cult of Personality." Reading further, we both became even more skeptical and called Mark immediately. "Anyone can write whatever they want online—it doesn't make it true. Stick it out until day three," he said. "Then decide for yourself. Be critical thinkers."

Until day three, I kept letting my white sash slip off during class. Incidentally, we received a lesson that third day about "suppressive" people, basically anyone who questioned any of the principles of the organization or wouldn't pay "tribute" to the founder Keith Raniere—Vanguard. Anytime you refused to acknowledge someone in a positive way or even go so far to take pleasure in their suffering, that was what ESP considered suppressive. In the real world, another word for suppressive would be "mean," like making jokes at another's expense or taking someone down in any way. In contrast, to pay tribute to Keith or to any senior member of the organization was to outwardly acknowledge what that person had accomplished in the world, or how they'd affected your own life. Acknowledging somebody's positive influence seemed normal enough, I figured. I just didn't totally get why they had to formalize it so much that it needed its own name.

Before I had the chance to examine this any further, one of the coaches explained to me privately that the organization distributed the white sashes on day one as an easy way to identify the angry "suppressives" who couldn't pay tribute or follow the philosophy. Right then I pretended to show a little more regard for my sash and go along with it.

In retrospect, I can see the coaches in the Five-Day were trying to weed out the followers who weren't going to be their sheep. Very early on in this training, Nancy also introduced the concept of what the community called a "parasite." This was someone who takes more than they produce in society, a company, community, or in any interpersonal scenario. They explained that the concept comes from the evolution of someone's psyche, because we all come into the world as parasites—babies—who literally feed off our mother's bodies as our "host." (Insightful? Yes. *Weird?* Also yes.) They taught us that by adulthood, there are two types of people: the "producers" who, metaphorically, are independent enough to pull themselves up to reach what they need; and the "parasites," who use emotionality such as whining, flirting, or getting sick, to get what they want. Keith was so against the "parasitic" type of individual that they offered Parasite I, II, and III as three different courses in the trainings. If there was a chance I was interested in pursuing this program, I knew I did not want to be considered a parasite.

We returned to our apartment at night, both exhausted and reeling from the amount of information we had just taken in. At the end of that first Five-Day, the seminar leaders said they were "promoting" each of us to one-stripe white, which means we each received one red stripe on our white sash because we'd completed the first training. But when they came to me, I found I was the only one in the class to receive two stripes because Suzanne had told our facilitators that I had enrolled David. Because of that, they said they would put him "under" me in the enrollment structure.

It felt like they saw something special in me. I kind of liked this path of earning; the satisfaction of having a clear goal and, if I'm being real, the most stripes of anyone in the room. I'd blown off the first couple days of the Five-Day intensive, but Mark had been right: by day three, I'd started having some big shifts and wondered what I could accomplish if I just tried this. I started to get excited about the Stripe Path and what it could do for my self-esteem and my sense of accomplishment. As an actor, I'd never had a path to measure my progress. I'd been working hard with acting, where there was no linear path forward as there is with many careers. Sometimes I booked a voiceover job; other times, a movie. You take what you can get. NXIVM felt like I'd finally discovered something I could stick to. I could learn to help others like the coaches had helped me.

We left on the final day in the manner Nancy had instructed us, paying tribute to NXIVM's founder, Keith, by bowing while saying, "Thank you, Vanguard." I felt self-conscious doing this, but we'd bowed and said these words after each time we recited the mission statement and at the close of each day in the training. At this point, it had come to feel less strange.

On the way home, I could sense David's unease with the social hierarchy, but I couldn't stop thinking about the lessons on self-esteem and how I'd been limiting my own possibilities. It was all so accurate.

As Nancy had guided us through written exercises, I'd also experienced a few "integrations," NXIVM's word for the breakthroughs that Oprah would call an "aha moment." Within a few days, I had broken a few of the reactionary patterns that I'd struggled with for years. Even David agreed with me that we actually wanted to bow to the mind that had created this material, so bowing to Vanguard had come to feel normal.

I returned home clearheaded about my goals and the fear that had been holding me back. I had heard people say things like "that's just the way I am." And now I had experienced tools that could really change people. Immediately I ended an unhealthy relationship with the agent who hadn't been getting me much work but whom I'd been afraid to sever ties with. I found a new one with a stronger reputation who sought out better opportunities for me and got me more auditions. I could hear assumptions and beliefs in people's languaging (a word I loved using!) and noticed I was communicating much more clearly and directly and navigating interpersonal challenges with much more grace and ease. Even though David still didn't always come to bed at the same time as I did every night, none of that stuff was really a big deal anymore.

These new ways of looking at things were indeed integrating into my everyday life. Mark was right. I'd learned that successful people see options and find a way to make it work. My whole life was beginning to make more sense.

I liken the experience of the Five-Day to the first time you take Bikram yoga. Put simply, it stinks . . . but as you get more familiar, you become used to the stench until you eventually don't even notice it. Afterward, it was like taking off sweaty, smelly yoga clothes and stepping into the shower: feeling lighter, fresher, so much stronger and clearer. Getting into the process sucked, but by the end, the benefit was so good.

After we left the Holiday Inn, I walked around feeling I had been given a book of secrets. I was living more consciously, with more awareness and authority in my actions and decisions. Even though my parents had raised me with the belief that I was in charge of my own destiny, the tools I'd learned in that Five-Day helped me to embody more license and assertiveness in my own life. I found that I could even stop taking sleeping pills—a crutch I'd relied on regularly for years.

I was seeing people and the world in a whole new light, and I wanted my loved ones to feel how I felt, and for us to engage in dialogues about this material. Fortunately, I found that a lot of my friends were receptive to learn more. After the Five-Day, I told the colleagues in my *Artist's Way* circle how the seminar had given me the real tools we all needed to succeed. Half the group joined me. The other half seemed a little skeptical. For some of them, it came down to money; but the others seemed to want to sit back and witness how this would work in my life before they'd jump in themselves.

They weren't the only ones. My mom listened to how excitedly I talked about ESP and hesitated to comment, but I thought I detected a little bit of question, even concern. My stepmom, whom my dad had married nearly twenty years earlier, was less discreet. For years she'd built a bond with me by doing arts and crafts sessions together, but when she told me she'd read that NXIVM was a cult, I dismissed her as being suppressive. "Really, Sarah?" she responded. "You think this Keith guy is a humanitarian? He's nothing but a greedy business-man!" Oh, right. Mark had prepped me for this, making the point that certain people won't like it when you suddenly make a drastic change in your life or habits. It would be hard for them to accept the new you. In the Five-Day the coaches had also warned us to be wary of the naysayers and told us not to believe what we read about NXIVM or Keith in the press. I was curious about what they were referring to, but more interested in aligning myself with these change makers. I thought my stepmom was just being negative. Why would she trust an article on the Internet instead of my experience? Our conversations were exhausting and frustrating.

In my first couple weeks following the Five-Day, I put these new principles into practice. I gave myself the permission to walk for hours and think them over, and felt I was gaining a better grasp on them. In those early weeks and months as I continued to read the material I'd received at the Five-Day and practice the exercises I'd learned, I grew passionate about this way of being. On the sincerest level, I was really starting to believe in it.

Later that year, a few of my close actress friends enrolled to take the Five-Day. We gathered to discuss our integrations and new awak-enings after that first workshop. When some of us started booking big-ger acting gigs, a few of our friends who'd watched from the sidelines decided they wanted to give it a try too. This became the foundation for the embrace of ESP by the acting community in Vancouver.

Through ESP, I was also beginning to meet new women—and a new *kind* of woman. These women were self-motivated and accom-plished business leaders. They earned their own living, supported them-selves, and did so while conducting work with a mission. The woman on the phone who had taken the remainder of my payment for my first Five-Day, Barbara Bouchey, was actually a lot warmer as I got to know her when she would enroll the friends I was bringing in. I learned that she'd had a successful career as a financial planner in the Capital Region of upstate New York, but she said she was outearning her old salary since she came on board to help Keith and Nancy grow NXIVM. "You've actually enrolled enough people to pursue the salesperson path," she informed me early on, adding that if I was good at sales, enrolling people could be a great avenue to be able to pay for more of my own trainings. She also explained that NXIVM had a unique employment structure that gave its own students the ability to earn a 20 percent commission for the other students they brought onboard. For example, if I brought a friend who paid $2,500 for the same Five-Day curriculum I attended, I would receive $500 from her enrollment. I thought about this . . . and it felt a little weird. "I'm not sure," I told Barbara. "I feel bad about the idea of making money off my friends."

"What's bad about it?"

I shrugged. "I don't know. It just doesn't feel right."

"Let's explore that," she said. Then she'd dig around to explore my reaction, asking me a series of questions. "Do you think the Five-Day is worth the cost?"

"Totally."

"Then why do you think money is bad, when you're providing a service of value? Why do you need your friends to perceive you a certain way? What do you make it mean?" These last six words were an ESP buzz phrase that was becoming familiar.

"Well," I said, realizing I'd never been pressed to closely analyze the basis of my friendships before. "I guess because . . . I want them to trust me."

"Interesting," she said. "Let's explore that." Barbara walked me through her matrix, where in perfect, memorized logic she explained the concept: "You receive money for a value you provide. Why is that bad?"

I listened; my brow furrowed as I worked to follow her reasoning.

"If you have created value in someone's life, then of *course* it's right for them to pay you for what you're providing to them. When you really think about it, it's like you're giving these life-changing principles away for free—it's just that someone's paying for the cost of putting on the training. Keith gives the tech away for free!"

Huh?

"I mean what's the price of this stuff?" she continued. "Exactly. See? You can't even answer. You know why? Because it's *priceless*." OK, *now* I was lost. "This material is reasonable, purposeful, and noble, and when you earn money for teaching it to others, you're upholding *your* highest values and gaining income for it. You've earned it! Does that make sense?"

Did that make sense? I'd never thought about it that way before. As I walked myself back through Barbara's design and repeated some of the steps of her reasoning back to myself, it was obviously a totally different way of looking at money. But then, wasn't that the point of this program—to view life and operate in it in a totally new way? I kept working it over in my head and began to feel more comfortable as I could see what Barbara had been saying. I'd been holding the limiting belief that desiring wealth was equivalent to greed, when it was just a fair measure of value. As I continued speaking with Barbara, she explained that I had just experienced another integration. I felt like I was catching on to this.

By now, the explorations of meaning—EMs—had become addictive, like my own version of "chasing the dragon." It was thrilling to make those discoveries about old reactionary patterns that hadn't been working for me, and the integrations had begun to give me a high. Ever since that first phone call with Mark on day one of my Five-Day, he encouraged all of us to ignore everything unfavorable that we'd ever heard or read about Keith Raniere. After all, Jesus, Buddha, and all other thought leaders met with resistance, he and the leaders explained, because most people in the world wanted things to stay status quo. Why else would human progress be necessary? They taught us a theory that came from the nineteenth-century German philosopher Schopenhauer: "All truth passes through three stages. First, it is ridiculed. Second, it is violently opposed. Third, it is accepted as being self-evident." Keith and the senior-level coaches believed that one day the teachings in ESP would be accepted by the general public as a way of life. It was exciting to consider being part of this movement in the world, so far ahead of the curve.

Which is why I didn't see Barbara's explanation of money as being manipulative. I knew the concept was . . . *different* from any prior understanding I'd had, but my questions at this time never reached a critical mass that led to doubt. If I had to choose one word to describe my attitude early on about this new kind of thinking, it would be *open*. Because a little more time would pass before I would understand NXIVM's recruitment and sales practices (and that they created a classic iteration of a pyramid scheme). I never thought to ask myself, *What's in it for her?* about Barbara's tactics or those of any of her colleagues. At this point it all seemed kosher. I wanted to believe that these people were purely good and that this was an evolved system of understanding life and walking in the world.

I'd quickly gone from dabbling in this to really exploring it. When Nancy—that is, Prefect—traveled from Albany to the West Coast a few days after my first Five-Day to attend the one-year anniversary of the Tacoma ESP center, Mark suggested I make the trip down to meet her.

While the meeting room at the Holiday Inn was underwhelming, the Tacoma ESP center was the first floor of a two-story home of two of the coaches who lived there. After five hours on the road and crossing the U.S. border, I walked through this stranger's home, passing her living room with grandma-style doilies on the end tables and teddy bears on the TV on my way to the meeting space. "You must be Sarah!" Nancy cried, coming over to hug me. "It's so good to finally meet you, Mark says you're like family!"

Wow, really? I'd only known Mark for a short time, and the fact that he would tell the president of this organization that he thought of me as fondly as a relative felt like such a compliment. "You're really going to have to meet my daughter, Lauren," she said. "She's about your age—wait, how old are you?"

"I'm twenty-eight."

She gasped. "Oh, come *on*. Lauren is twenty-eight, too!" She continued, such speed in her words as she told me all the reasons she was sure Lauren and I would hit it off: we were both Jewish, we both loved theater, and we both had moms who were therapists—"Poor things," Nancy said, throwing back her head in laughter.

"Does Lauren live in Albany, too?" I asked.

"Yes. You should really come see us there."

See them there? Wow. That felt like an invitation. I was starting—just *starting*—to feel that these could indeed be my people. The women from the Tacoma center asked us all to be seated, and I felt drawn to sit near Nancy. As I made my way to the front as a keen new student, one of the senior coaches pulled me aside to remind me about "rank order." In the Five-Day, we learned that the senior-level coaches, like the green sashes and the two purples, always sat in the front of any audience, closest to Keith if he was in attendance. The lower-level students, like us white sashes, were relegated to the back. The group of women from the Tacoma center stood in a line before us, and then broke into song:

Because I knew you,
I have been changed for good . . .

It was one of my favorite songs of all time, from *Wicked*. And I *wanted* to like this—I wanted to embrace them. Nancy looked on with dramatic reverence as the Tacoma women shed tears while they sang to her, but all I felt was embarrassment. I got it: it was a really big deal to have Prefect at their center (though I was generally continuing to call her Nancy because her NXIVM title felt so uncomfortable to say). As the women belted out the song, I wondered: were they really proud to do this? Something just didn't feel right.

In NXIVM, a demonstration like this was a perfect example of what the leaders called "paying tribute." This practice of group worship was highly encouraged anytime you encountered or were introducing one of the senior-level figures. But for now, I focused on staying positive about all of this and open to everything new that ESP was exposing me to. Mark had said I was like family. The principles I was learning had begun to lead to integrations, and in turn, the members I knew—Mark Vicente and now Nancy, these two successful influencers—were inviting me to become part of their community. I felt a sense of belonging and of being part of a team, which I'd always wanted.

I wanted to believe that this work was truly transformational. I also pondered how I'd already hit it off pretty naturally with Nancy and Mark, who were two of the most influential figures in the community. As long as Mark made himself available to David and me anytime we felt uncertainty, I'd continue to remain committed—and anytime I had started to feel some doubt, it was Mark who reminded me that any worthwhile progress always starts with questions.

That promise about evolving humanity was how the senior-level executives made sure those of us who seemed like good targets would want to stay in. In passing conversations during the Five-Day and now here in Tacoma, I'd heard the senior coaches compare Keith Raniere to Steve Jobs and Bill Gates—leaders who saw the world differently and inspired millions everywhere to live their lives by totally different everyday practices. And for those leaders, they reminded us, there were always haters. There'd been the people who said computers would never become mainstream. The ones who said iTunes ruined the film and music businesses (I knew people in my industry who felt that way). But, the senior coaches reminded us, hadn't these magnates brought ideas to fruition that changed the way people lived? The world *needed* to change, and our ethics needed to evolve to match our current technology. Most people just hadn't realized it yet. NXIVM was driving a shift in collective thinking.

Ultimately, despite all of the weirdness, I came away after meeting Nancy feeling really good. The curriculum and the tools transcended any doubts I had at the time. I had also accepted the notion that any discomfort was an area for growth . . . and I wanted to grow more than I wanted anything. Maybe, just maybe, this was the path and community I'd been seeking all my life.

CHAPTER THREE

INNER DEFICIENCY

JULY 2005
ALBANY, NEW YORK

The three months after my Five-Day had been the happiest and most productive time I'd ever experienced in my life. David and I were waking up early, following through on our goals, and attacking life with a passion and consistency I'd never known was possible. He was writing scripts in incredibly short windows of time, and I was feeling grounded and confident at auditions. I noticed I wasn't reactive to one-on-one issues that previously would have sent me into a tailspin. My "monkey mind," as I always called my propensity to overthink, was still when I went to bed at night. I had such clarity in my interactions and a vision for my life that people had begun to ask me: "What are you doing differently? What is your secret?"

David and I were excited to finish the initial introductory curriculum, known as the Sixteen-Day, by following up the Five-Day with an eleven-day intensive. The problem was that these Eleven-Days were usually based in Albany. Barbara Bouchey had told me: "The Five-Day is just the beginning. It's like going in for surgery and getting all washed and prepped and scrubbed and opened up. The Eleven-Day will go in and extract that tumor!" Another winning analogy from Barbara, but all of the coaches had stressed that the best was yet to come when you finished the training by taking the Eleven-Day.

So three months after the Five-Day, David and I flew for the first time from Vancouver to Albany to attend the remaining days with

Mark Vicente and his girlfriend. Mark had asked us to join them in completing the first full level of training. I felt like we were all intellectual partners in this. At the conclusion of the Eleven-Day, our first level of official ESP training would be complete. Once we'd completed Level I, we could advance to Level II trainings. These covered more profound concepts that apparently we hadn't touched in the beginner classes. We were both ready to level up.

I was excited, and *maybe* a little intimidated, to learn alongside Mark. The endgame was that I wanted to learn *from* him, because deep down, I was hoping that at some point he might want to work with David, or me, or both of us. Mark was the one who'd urged us to check out NXIVM, and I couldn't wait to have exchanges with him about some of these new concepts, and about progress in our lives and careers in general.

I was also looking forward to talking with Mark about how the Five-Day had already impacted my life; how I'd begun to identify all the ways that I'd been willing to live with my shortcomings for years. Now I felt more ambitious. I was handling my relationships with my family and my boyfriend with a lighter grip than ever before, and no one could believe how much calmer and less anxious I seemed. Even the apartment was more organized. Now I'd taken the same curriculum Mark had. Barbara Bouchey, the field trainer who had processed my final payment for the Five-Day on the phone, offered to cover my fee for the Eleven-Day because she believed I could earn that money back by enrolling many friends to take the Five-Day. Already, I had three friends back in Vancouver who had expressed interest. I hoped Mark would be pleased to hear that I was working to bring friends in, and that I was incorporating the tools from the Five-Day in my life. David would still have to pay, but again—for both of us—this was a great opportunity for some face time with Mark.

We were sharing a rental car with him and renting affordable rooms from other students of the program. It seemed like a smart arrangement to me, and besides, I was interested to meet other Espians (the community's term for ESP students).

When we'd checked into our housing and headed toward the training facility in our rental car, I took note of the area during the brief drive through a wooded suburb to NXIVM's offices. The energy of the place didn't feel particularly pulsing as we passed a number of small shopping plazas, gas stations, and the airport. Maybe the training facility itself would have a little more of a wow factor.

We turned off a main road into a driveway toward the address we'd been given: 455 New Karner Road. I could dismiss the surroundings and remember the way I felt as we left the car and made our way inside a nondescript one-story brick office building: I was part of something. A team. An allegiance. It was a feeling I'd never experienced before . . . and something I'd wanted since I was young.

But while that Five-Day near Vancouver had come almost too easily in equipping me with a feeling of empowerment, at the Eleven-Day in Albany, something happened that I never would have been able to anticipate. First, we recited the NXIVM mission statement that we'd first gone over at the Five-Day and had recited again in Tacoma in our binders from Staples. This time, we were reading off a giant poster-board version, which stood on a high tripod at the front of the room. The words weren't new to me, but as the training started, it felt like the curriculum in the Eleven-Day had been designed to strip us down to nothing. Everything we learned at this training provided a sharp contrast to the life I'd been living. Inside that intensive, I learned that none of my values were real, but were only important to me in covering up my inability to really know or love myself.

I'd shown up an eager pupil, but just a short while into the first day I found myself holding back from participating. The material was focused on drilling down to the base assumption that everything we do is driven by a deficiency—not by our good nature or any altruistic virtue. *But I've always liked to help others*, I thought. If a group of friends went on a camping trip and someone was hungry, I would pull out a granola bar. If someone needed a Band-Aid, a hair elastic, or some dental floss, I loved being the one to pull it from my purse. An exercise encouraged us to write a word we'd use to describe ourselves. *I'm helpful*, I scribbled down. But by the end of the exercise, I'd realized: *I'm not helpful! I use people to feel good about myself!*

According to the ESP material, helping others was what gave me my worth. Even my acting career had been a pursuit driven by my need for attention . . . not because I wanted to promote positivity in the world.

Each day was a different topic such as Anger, Fear, Control, Right/Wrong, Ethics, and Relationships. We would spend hours on modules, EMs, and other exercises. We learned that dependency on anything in the outside world to feel complete points to your deficiency and needs to be addressed as nothing from the outside will fill that void.

The first two days are really uncomfortable, I remembered Mark saying about the Five-Day. Uncomfortable? The Eleven-Day was beyond.

I tried to catch David's eye, and Mark's, but both of them were locked into the material. I looked around for anything or anyone that felt familiar. Nancy wasn't here; in fact, I'd overheard a couple of the trainers whispering that she was away giving a talk about bioethics in Mexico. By now I'd learned that Nancy had provided ESP training to figures like the executive team at Enron, as well as Antonia Novello, the first female and Hispanic surgeon general of the United States, and Edgar Bronfman Sr., the billionaire heir to the Seagram's liquor fortune. Every moment of doubt I felt was countered with some reason to hang in there, even weakly. I wanted to be part of this league. The Five-Day had helped erase so much of my self-doubt; I had not been expecting to feel it more than ever here. But if this eleven-day seminar was my test, I wasn't about to quit—especially not in front of Mark and the rest of the class.

As we neared the end of the intensive, the trainers said we should prepare ourselves to write our own mission statement, for our life. *A mission statement?* I had spent the last week asking myself what the fuck I'd been doing for the last twenty-eight years. I had no self-love, no idea of who I was, and the only thing I felt confident in knowing was that everything I'd done until this point was to cover up my deficient need to be liked. How could I write a mission statement for my life?

As I struggled through the worksheets and questions the leaders posed to us, everyone else in the course seemed to be flying through with ease. I felt sweat spike through my scalp as I wondered whether maybe I'd received a different version of the material than everybody else. Why were they doing the assignment so effortlessly?

I watched as the other students all around me pondered the written material thoughtfully, calmly, as they productively jotted down notes. Even my friends here looked like they were enjoying the process. Mark worked. His girlfriend was relaxed. David showed a level of engagement I never would have anticipated from him given how he'd reacted to the Five-Day. During breaks, they all stretched back with smiles, took short walks into the hallway, and engaged in lighthearted conversation. *Where are you from? What do you do? Where did you take the Five-Day?*

I tried to appear at ease but wondered: Was everybody else just so ready to face their personal flaws? Why did I feel like I was the only one who was seriously jarred by some of the findings we were uncovering about ourselves?

The last thing I could have guessed was that my reaction to the tech was exactly what the coaches were looking for. As it turned out, in their eyes my sensitivity to the curriculum actually strengthened my potential as a candidate for becoming a "lifer" with ESP. The material in the Eleven-Day schooled us in the notion that everything, *everything*, we'd been doing in our career paths and interpersonal relationships was to fill a specific void—what they called our "inner deficiency." For an actress like me whose career came with the inherent requisite of earning others' approval just to land work and pay the bills, this idea of an inner deficiency hit me in a really tender spot. For as long as I could remember, I'd held some suspicion that there'd always been something fundamentally wrong with me. I also knew this belief made me more uptight and judgmental of myself than almost anyone I knew.

The head coach in the Eleven-Day taught us that all our past ways of operating had been developed around this deficiency, and that system of behavior was getting in the way of everything we really wanted. They explained one of Keith Raniere's principal beliefs: that all we humans really need to survive are food, water, shelter, and air. Anything else—clothes, connection, love, money, relationships—were pure "desires," or "nonintegrated fixations"—things we thought we needed to be happy, whole, and complete, but that were ultimately just cover-ups for our inner deficiencies.

Hang on a second: we didn't need money to live? And from all the years I'd taken an interest in literature, the humanities, and psychology . . . weren't humans social creatures who needed interaction for our emotional well-being? They explained that true enlightenment is the ability to live with only the basics. Keith, they said, was a renunciate, meaning he owned no material possessions, and celibate—he didn't have sex or any romantic affiliations.

Of course I didn't know that this extreme construct around a basic understanding of values is a powerful way that cults prep new members so that their own values and beliefs won't come into conflict with the cult's mission (which is almost always to deify one person—in this case, Keith Raniere).

They introduced one segment of tech called Blame & Responsibility, the only module taught in both the Five-Day and the Eleven-Day. In essence, according to ESP teachings, blaming is a proactive attempt to prove you have no responsibility in a given situation. Taking responsibility, on the other hand, is attempting to recognize your participation in all things, whether you want to see it or not. Acknowledging how you might be causing it is the first step in resolving it. Taking responsibility was somewhat synonymous with being at-cause.

The Eleven-Day gave us more tools to be at-cause. I could ask myself, *If something negative happens to me, how did I participate in it? How could I have avoided it?* An example that Nancy introduced was that if you were to get hit by a car, what role would you have played? Well, easy: *you* had stepped out in front of the car. *Ouch*, I thought. This perspective definitely gave a new spin to the way I'd always thought about being hit by a car. We were encouraged to think about it this way: if you made it the driver's fault that you got struck, or the city's fault for engineering their streets in a way that made it conducive for you to get hit, then you granted those parties more "potency," or power, in the relationship with you. While the car example might have seemed extreme, when I applied this same thought process to everyday situations, it called me to own my part in any scenario or interaction and then choose wiser the next time I was confronted with a similar set of circumstances. Just noting these distinctions built awareness that I could choose differently. To see it this way would be impossible if you operated by a blaming mentality.

All this clicked for me: if I had blamed David for making me feel unloved because he hadn't come to bed when I did, then I had asserted that he was a more powerful individual than I was, giving him potency over my feelings and state of being. Now I had the clear awareness that by using this process, I could choose differently and evolve most situations.

Nancy also introduced the concept of "state control." This came from the school of thought known as neurolinguistics programming (NLP), which was one of the foundations of Nancy's career. State control is the idea that we humans have ultimate control over our moods and emotions—our "states"—and that people can't *make* us feel anything that we don't want or allow ourselves to feel. No more blaming others for making us feel a certain way. We are in control, and with practice, we can choose how we want to feel at any moment and bring up that emotion at will. We learned how to quickly access, anchor, and self-trigger different states, such as motivation, excitement, power, and magnificence. A real-life example of using state control is someone triggering a motivated state to shake off a lethargic mood in order to finish a work project on time. I would later find this incredibly useful in my acting and voiceover career.

To be *at-cause* was one of ESP's four pillars. The other three were:

- *work-value*, which is to elucidate what your supposed values are and to define value as that which saves time and effort and moves humanity forward. Anything good builds value and is pro-survival. Anything bad destroys value and is counter-survival.

- *honesty and disclosure*, that it's incumbent upon an individual to own your values and your filters so you can become self-aware and understand how you're making decisions, and what mechanisms in all of us inform how we make those decisions.

- and *projection*, or your own interpretation of circumstances and events. We were called to understand that you can never know what's going on in someone else's mind, so anything you perceive about them is viewed through the lens of your own life. Rather than making a blanket assumption that *they're this way*, realizing *I'm projecting their way of being, and I may or may not be right*.

The first time I really understood this concept was not till a few months later when I got an EM about my "right/wrong" issues. I brought the coach a situation where I felt really *right*. Like viscerally. I had been carpooling down to Ethos in Tacoma and asked one of the coaches for a ride back to Vancouver. As we were crossing the border she asked which corner I would like to be dropped off on and I had a huge reaction about her not taking me to my home—especially because it was midnight! The exploration allowed me to see that I was not taking responsibility for being more specific when I had asked her for a ride in the first place—or for my emotional reaction—blaming her for my upset. The sourcing and the concepts around blame allowed me to transition out of any interpersonal dynamic with grace and ease. My triggers were rapidly diminishing and my communication skills were so much better. This was one example of how ESP's teachings would bring us to examine the nitty-gritty of our words, thoughts, behaviors, and decisions. They called on us Espians to be conscious of *everything* we did or said. I knew if I stuck with this, there would be no aspect of life left to gloss over. When it came to every choice, ESP would call me to have eyes in the back of my head.

My worry at this stage was that I was already plenty self-aware. I didn't have the distance from my habit of self-inquiry to view these scenarios objectively. Instead, I began to take the new insights personally.

The principles in the Eleven-Day put me on edge but were also easy for me to follow because they reinforced all the doubts and dislikes I'd always had about myself. In truth, I *was* known to experience anger even as far back as my teen years. Yes, I did sometimes feel the need to control outcomes in my career and relationships. I did some-times seek feedback from others in order to feel more secure about myself. In a way, I'd always been very independent—but, I mean, not *totally* independent. Sometimes it just made me feel better to have support from others . . . and in a way, isn't that what friends and loved ones were for?

As I moved through this coursework and overheard some of the coaches chatting and laughing among themselves during breaks, I wondered what their world must be like. One had mentioned her love for going on hours-long walks with Keith and her colleagues, where they would engage in deep conversations about life, the state of the community, and the direction of the company. Everybody with a green sash seemed to have a close working relationship with Keith. I could see that leadership in the company and community was closely tied with having Keith's approval.

As I observed our leaders throughout the eleven-day course, I learned that they were all vegetarian, into organic foods and chemical-free products. They were fit. They meditated, didn't get drunk (or drink at all), and got together often to celebrate their wins. This was a tight-knit group. These women were also badass—they had powerful careers, influential roles in the company. I'd already gotten the impression that Nancy Salzman was constantly flying around the country to present workshops to figures too famous for her to reveal them by name.

These women embodied many of my own ideals. What could life be like on this path? It seemed like they lived in their own utopia with daily practices and a community that supported their purposes, along with their inner peace. I'd been educated, had lived on my own, had lived *with* someone, and had even spent a gap year before university traveling in Israel. Through these varied experiences, I'd developed my notion of what my creature comforts were . . . but could it be worth shedding these "nonintegrated fixations," as ESP referred to our attachments, to experience this seemingly enlightened lifestyle?

I began to view my life through this new lens to comprehend that my desire to be liked had driven everything. Guess who offered the tools to fix that?

The trainers claimed that if we made it through the Eleven-Day, we would have completed Level I of the Executive Success Program. At that point, the course offerings in the Level II trainings could provide a framework for me to really grow and learn to fill that void for myself, instead of looking for external validation . . . for just a few thousand more dollars.

At the time, I didn't see that NXIVM itself was becoming my response to the stimulus-response pattern they taught us about, or that I was turning to NXIVM to fill that same inner void. I pressed on with the early courses and trusted the system. All the processes packed into those intensive eleven days had worked up a lot of my old "stuff." I felt raw, exposed, exhausted. The others seemed to have breezed through the material with curiosity and ease. I still felt like something was wrong with me.

This trip was also the first time I would meet Keith Raniere in person. I encountered him during a NXIVM volleyball game, which I had heard was one of his favorite activities. I'd never been the athletic type and wasn't keen on participating in the game . . . especially as I looked around at the people on the court. They were mostly men playing and on the sideline sat beautiful young women in very short shorts who all seemed into the sport. Between sets, Keith would pause to greet or check in with some of the women. *Wait, is he kissing all of them on the lips?* In his Jesus hair, glasses, and early 1980s shorts, Keith—I mean Vanguard—bantered with them casually and seemed to preen in their attention as they all tittered at a joke he made. I watched with uncertainty as he shook his shaggy hair away from his forehead and briefly met my gaze.

Then, during a break between games, Mark Vicente made the introduction between Keith, David, and me. I stuck out my hand to greet him and thanked him for creating the tech, aware of how awkward I must have seemed even as the words came out of my mouth. It seemed as though he had already heard about David and me, and I felt sort of flattered, but the interaction was odd. I took off to follow David, who had already moved away from the court.

After this first encounter with Keith, it would take me a couple minutes to put my finger on the way I felt. I'd expected to feel awestruck or intimidated . . . but more than anything, I found him weird. It also struck me as odd that one of the smartest people in the world would be playing something as normal, even pedestrian, as volleyball. Mark had told me that Keith was an accomplished classical pianist, a competitive chess player, and an avid reader. I guess I'd been expecting us all to gather into some intellectual circle and engage in a groundbreaking discussion about the state of the world.

My first impression was that he was totally normal. Not a genius, and kind of a schlub. Later I noted that after every forum that Keith held, Nancy would follow his time on stage by debriefing the audience and saying: "How was that for everyone? Wasn't he fantastic?" There would always be some new student who would put up their hand and say, "Yeah, I am surprised about how he comes across as just a guy," and Nancy would always gush, "Isn't it amazing how accessible he makes himself?"

As the Eleven-Day came to a close, I felt like the lone outsider. While everyone else was writing their mission statements and life's purpose, I sat curled up on my chair, wiping tears away in embarrassment and keeping my face down toward my binder, which I used as a hard surface to write on. I desperately wanted to ask one of the coaches for help. I didn't know how to do the exercise. At the front of the room, one of the coaches announced that it wasn't uncommon for people to become emotional during a training, so I *knew* they saw what I was experiencing, but I felt particularly abandoned. In the previous exercise, I had just identified that I expressed love by helping people . . . so I felt that because no one was helping me, I was unlovable. They'd also told us that the Stripe Path was the "science of joy," but examining my issues so closely and with so much focus had brought me into a state of misery. I reminded myself that I wasn't being graded, that this was all for my growth. . . . But if I couldn't write my mission statement, then what would I have to aim for from this point? I wrote a few lines as best I could and sat inconspicuously while a few other students rose to share their mission statements out loud.

Then I met Lauren. During a break in the training when David and I wandered into the center's café to grab something to drink, I spoke to one of the other Espians I'd just met, named Clare. "Excuse me," I said. "I'm just looking for the recycling bin."

"We don't recycle at any of the NXIVM centers," she told me, wrinkling her nose to push up her thick glasses. She said Keith didn't believe in it; that he thought it was a "shifter strategy."

In the Five-Day, we had learned the NXIVM principle of the "shifter." Keith Raniere's philosophy was that a shifter is an individual or a corporation that creates a problem and uses it to profit from the solution, which they also offer. An example that had been used in class was big pharma—often the companies that sell you pesticides that make you sick will also sell you the cure to your sickness. Keith actually pantomimes picking up litter outside, Clare told me.

What?

She went on to explain that Keith refused to support shifters and felt it was unethical to clean up after people because then you were teaching them that it was OK to litter. She added that to make sure he wasn't avoiding effort and appearing lazy, Keith would pantomime picking up garbage from the street to demonstrate for others that we shouldn't be lazy, meanwhile refusing to enable litterbugs.

Some of this stuff is so inconsistent, I thought. *What am I not getting?* And then I spotted her.

Lauren Salzman had the profile of a young Barbra Streisand. She wore a green sash, which meant she'd already advanced as far up the Stripe Path as any leader could go other than the one blue and two purple sashes. It was inspiring that somebody my age had already made it that far.

But at the same time, she seemed relatable and really cool. When she introduced herself to me, I noted that her shoulder-length hair was tied back in—wait, was that a scrunchy? "I'm trying to bring these back into fashion," she told me, rolling her eyes with a playful grin. I instantly liked her sense of humor and that she didn't take herself too seriously. Nancy had already told me a lot about how much her daughter had accomplished, but I'd had no idea what to expect. Now, in person, I felt both a great deal of respect and an instant kinship with her—and for the first time, I relaxed.

As we chatted, I eased up and felt a renewed sense of hope similar to what I'd felt when I received my white sash with two red stripes: that I could do this.

I paid attention to Lauren's mannerisms, her jewelry—minimalist, but pretty—her clothes, a baggy tunic T-shirt and jeans. I watched her closely as she spoke. She wasn't pretentious and didn't act like she had it all figured out. She was casual, cute . . . Lauren was real.

She asked me how the training was going for me, and I admitted that the Five-Day material had come easily, but here I was finding myself in an unexpected struggle. She quieted herself, really listening as I spoke.

I felt myself watching Lauren's every move, so wanting her to be the person I could lean on to guide me through this journey and help me feel safe. And she did. Assuring me that she too had encountered questions and challenges when she started the program, she offered support and encouragement. Her mom had mentioned me to her, she said, and the senior levels were really seeing potential in me. "Let's grab lunch sometime," she said.

"For sure!" With that, I could have dashed back into the classroom. It was exactly what I'd needed to hear.

It seemed as if now that Lauren had taken an interest in getting to know me, the other coaches were starting to come around a little more. One of them crouched next to me to talk me through the next exercise, and I started to feel confident enough to strike up conversations with the other Espians during breaks. If I warmed up to all this a little more and even had a chance to get to know Lauren, maybe this group could be a safety nest of support where I could grow and become the fully developed person I wanted to be.

Over the course of the past week and a half, I'd gotten to see how the leaders of the community were so committed to the program and how self-assured it had made them. Now, as this small group gathered around me in the midst of the grueling training exercises, any apprehension I had felt about the program was alleviated. I'd always felt that being myself and showing vulnerability was a turnoff to people, but here I'd bared my soul. The attention they'd just begun to show me during the most brutal moments of the Eleven-Day further deepened my feeling that they saw something worthwhile in me that I couldn't see.

I remembered the "urge to bolt" thing that Nancy had referred to at the beginning of the Five-Day. If I was actually going to change, then maybe I did have to fix my deficiencies, become the ideal me, and stick with the program.

CHAPTER FOUR

MASTER TEACHER

AUGUST 2005

Even if I'd listened to my "urge to bolt," by then it was too late. The executives in NXIVM had scheduled that Eleven-Day in August 2005 to roll conveniently into Vanguard Week, their annual ten-day retreat celebrating Keith Raniere's birthday. Hundreds of Espians from across the United States and the four centers in Mexico would attend V-Week, as the more veteran members were calling the event. It would be held at Silver Bay, a rustic resort about ninety minutes north of Albany on Lake George in the gorgeous Adirondack Mountains.

There was one little problem for David and me: after maxing out our credit cards on the Five-Day in Vancouver and one admission to the Eleven-Day intensive in Albany, we couldn't afford to attend V-Week. How could I continue to be part of this utopian micro-society while living on a limited budget? I learned that when NXIVM really wanted you, they'd find a way.

As David and I were considering going to the Eleven-Day and I'd explained our financial quandary to Mark, he said he might be able to work out a solution. Later that same day, he called me back and said the senior leaders were offering to let us attend V-Week for free, if David and I would commit to what Mark was calling a "work exchange."

The agreement was this: since Mark Vicente had agreed to shoot the entire ten-day experience on camera, David would join his camera team. I, in turn, would come on as David's assistant, carrying gear, setting up lighting, labeling tapes, and being a Jane of all trades. Sure, I had worked in productions for several years, but I hesitated to reveal that I was totally unequipped for this. I'd had *zero* training in any kind of technical production work. David and I felt the same way: we didn't want to miss out on V-Week and the chance to work with Mark. Learning from Mark Vicente would be so enriching; and, gullible about this arrangement, we were impressed at the extraordinary lengths the NXIVM executives were willing to go to in order to have us there. Plus, a star from one of the biggest American soap operas of all time was planning to attend. This would clearly be good company, *and* again, while other Espians paid a few thousand dollars to attend, David and I were going for free. It was nice to feel so included.

I learned that because the organization was still building, they were often willing to accept this type of "work exchange" as payment from attendees: if you were a professional in a certain field that could provide services or a product they needed, they might be willing to forgo your monetary payment.

Before this, I had never seen a corporation employ individuals' skills for anything other than profit. What the executives in NXIVM were willing to do for us seemed like the perfect mutually beneficial arrangement. That really appealed to me about this community: even if you didn't have money you could pay, they made it possible for you to contribute something of value so that you could participate. To me, this was proof that they were committed to helping me grow and saw quality in what David and I brought to the community. That—combined with this weeklong opportunity to network with other professionals—would go a long way.

For several years in my career I'd felt that I'd been throwing myself at influential decision-makers to show them my skills. Here, it felt like this community saw potential in my talent and were putting it to use.

I was relieved to find that while the Eleven-Day had been tough, V-Week was mostly inspiring. These ten days weren't totally jam-packed with intense learning like the Five-Day and Eleven-Day; instead, this was way more recreational, with a few optional training modules scheduled each day. It was like summer camp for grown-ups and families, plus modules taught by Nancy in the flesh instead of videos. As the three of us followed Vanguard around the property, it was fun to watch the participants—more than three hundred of them—playing sports, spending time outdoors, and rehearsing for the talent show that would be one of the finales to the week.

I loved the sunrise hikes, the pre-breakfast yoga flow. The EMs with higher-ranking coaches on the porch. The dance classes taught by a professional choreographer from Mexico who had worked on huge events like the opening ceremonies of the Pan-American games. The children playing freely, progressive moms and dads who spoke to their children like the small humans they were. At night, everyone filed into an auditorium while small groups of Espians presented skits or other performances as tribute to Vanguard. Here, the tributes were more humorous than serious, but still . . . I wondered why one man needed to receive so much attention. I took the neutral approach of a journalist as David, Mark, and I worked. New to the scene, I observed the crowd as Keith laughed at the presentations onstage: lip syncs, dances, goofy costumes—people essentially making fools of themselves to poke fun at their own "issues" and express gratitude for what he'd done in their lives. One called Keith "the most noble man I've ever met," and I couldn't decide whether I found all the unabashed tributes to Keith nauseating or inspiring. What I did know is that I didn't want to be called "suppressive" in front of all these new faces when I was still trying to figure things out. Then, they called Clare Bronfman's sister, Sara, before the audience and promoted her to green sash. I stood back as the crowd cheered for her, wondering whether one day I could possibly make my way that far up the Stripe Path.

We followed Keith around as he presented before the full audience of hundreds in the evening forums and spoke in private with his executives and several of the V-Week attendees. As he sat down in front of the lights and camera to share his thoughts and philosophies, it amazed me that despite the misfortune of our limited budget, David and I had been chosen to serve as his entourage that week. With the production crew surrounding him, I could begin to view him in the way that hadn't clicked for me in our previous encounter at the volleyball game. He clearly enjoyed receiving attention but also had a kind, powerful way of fixing on an individual in conversation that could make you feel like you were the only one there. And while I couldn't have described him as *humble*, exactly, this time he came across with more charisma, even likability, than the impression I'd first gotten.

As Vanguard conveyed some of his philosophies before the camera, he had a way of introducing an idea and then following the thought with curiosity to develop a conclusion, as if the question we'd posed was leading him on a stroll through the woods. He visibly enjoyed being upheld as the one with all the answers, but there was a glimmer in his eye when he spoke as if he found it entertaining to be regarded in this way.

That week I sat in on several lessons presented by Nancy Salzman—er, Prefect. While her delivery continued to be giddy, when Keith spoke, his presence was jovial and down-to-earth. He tucked his hair behind his ears and used his hands to make points, as if plucking a thought out of thin air. He had a boyish way of nervously biting his lip just before offering answers as he expounded on topics ranging from creativity to productivity to ethics to science.

The thing was, I couldn't follow what the hell he was saying in either of the forums that happened during this first V-Week. I might glean a couple nuggets of wisdom, but mostly I was lost. When Mark asked him a question about quantum physics and dark matter, Keith's answer somehow shifted into how science has no free will. A question about the development of thought was met with an answer about something entirely unrelated. The senior levels asserted that Keith's genius was a template to help anyone with their goals, regardless of the content, whether an individual had enrolled to get better at hockey, horse jumping, making more money, or whatever. Keith definitely seemed to have a great deal of confidence in the way he'd formed these ideas. At the time, I thought maybe they were just beyond me. I would find out later about a concept called "word salad," a scramble of nonsense words put together with no particular sequence or meaning. Keith spoke in these highbrow, philosophical terms so that no one could follow him on purpose.

That first V-Week we worked around the clock and on call, because Keith often slept late and then after everyone had gone to bed would feel some inspiration to have us shoot him while he explored some new idea as it was coming to him. We filmed him at all hours of the night, sometimes at a moment's notice. He was insistent that we capture his every thought. We'd been told that all of these musings, forums, and teachings were being catalogued for a "Vanguard database," which still kind of puzzled me.

At one point after a forum I got tired and retreated to the back of the auditorium to snack on an apple. Seconds after Nancy had left the stage, she stood at my side. "You're not supposed to eat during trainings," she said.

"Oh," I replied. "I'm sorry. I didn't realize that a forum is a training."

"You're mad-dogging me," she said. My stomach dropped. "Next time you're hungry or tired, I would advise you to change your state."

This was another red flag that first V-Week; in particular those tributes to Keith and Nancy and the overdone "rah rah"-ness of the whole vibe. In a crowd, I sought out Lauren and confessed that I was having a struggle, as they called a reaction in the program. "Let's go look at that," she'd say, leading me away from the group activity so the two of us could find a quiet spot on the porch. As we moved through the exploration, I followed her instruction with total trust. I revealed memories from my past, and she coached me on the practices I could use to unhook the beliefs that might have been creating roadblocks for me. She asked a series of eye-opening questions:

"Think about any time in your life. Is there somebody you've struggled with—even if it's someone you love?"

"Yes," I said. "My stepmother."

"What does that person do that creates struggle for you?"

"She's negative and doesn't stand behind a lot of my goals."

"How do you need her to be different in order for you to feel better?"

"She could be more supportive."

This led to a huge discovery: I needed an outer circumstance (my stepmom's support) to change in order to experience an inner feeling of strength and confidence in who I ultimately wanted to be—and, most powerfully, I could adopt that state of being right now, independent of any external circumstance.

"Do you see how this person is a master teacher to bring this confusion to light? Do you see how you're projecting your experiences onto this person so that each time you react to them, it's just you not yet being where you want to be?"

Whoa . . . In this exercise, I learned that anyone who exposes our deficiency is a master teacher and someone we can thank for the growth opportunity.

This is one taste of the way I found the tech effective and insightful in the early days. As the exercise came to a close, I only wished it had been more of a dialogue; that I wasn't the only one baring my soul. I wanted to know Lauren as well as she was coming to know me. Had she ever felt the way I was feeling? She didn't volunteer much about her experience, but as she coached me, she seemed to have a very personal understanding of a lot of what I was saying. Her way of teaching was so gentle in its insights, never critical. She was the head trainer who was the most skilled and likable . . . and, I felt, she was also a trustworthy friend.

I had found a confidante, someone who would listen and understand and look out for me. I was still working to figure things out and unwinding from the whirlwind that had been my first foray into the "inner circle." At V-Week, I'd felt valued for my work, even though I also felt overworked. Some things seemed over the top, but whenever they did, I'd found I had Lauren to go to. And the EMs and breakthroughs kept coming. So even though some of the teachings were over my head and the groupthink and activities felt exaggerated, because of my connection with Mark it felt less like I was one of the masses and more like I was involved with the right people. Any doubts were always trumped by the tech and the integrations I was having, in combination with the pleasure of working alongside Mark. If I wanted to produce work that would change the world, I had to have faith I was on the right path.

And as long as I had Lauren and Mark, I believed I could find the strength to keep moving forward.

CHAPTER FIVE

FALL 2005

At this point, after completing the Five-Day and the Eleven-Day and working with Mark at V-Week, I felt like I was in. David and I had invested time, energy, and money to travel from western Canada to the East Coast of the United States for the trainings. We'd begun to develop real relationships with people in the company, and I'd seen that most of the other students who had advanced significantly on the Stripe Path had picked a favorite head trainer to follow and would attend all of the intensives that head trainer taught. In order to grow in the organization, my plan was to learn from the only gold sash: Nancy.

So during that fall of 2005, I arrived in Albany for the second time in three months with Nicki Clyne, a fellow Canadian actress from my *Artist's Way* group who had taken note of my progress and was interested in the Five-Day. Nicki was young but making strides in her career, having starred for the past two years in a hit American TV show. I'd met her a few months earlier while we were both on an audition for a Dentyne commercial. We weren't super-close friends, but Nicki was a thinker and really smart, and I had a feeling she'd like ESP. Nicki seemed like the perfect person to share this with, and now, all I needed was one more recruit to attend the Five-Day at NXIVM's headquarters in Albany for free.

Bingo. Also accompanying us on the cross-continental journey was my mother, who made it clear that she was coming along mostly to inspect this program that I was getting into. I'll admit this made me a *little* nervous—but Nancy Salzman was going to be there, and I hoped that maybe they would hit it off as Lauren and I had. It was, in fact, my mom who had introduced me to the concept of personal growth in the first place, so I was excited to share these new tools with her. I hoped they would both help her with her health and bond our relationship further.

My mother is incredibly nurturing and soft-spoken, but she has a disarming way of expressing her questions or doubts. There were a few moments during the Five-Day when I found myself whispering desperately: "Mom, please *stop* it." I was embarrassed that my mom wasn't willing to accept the teachings more easily. Based on some of the questions she was asking inside the seminar, I could tell that she wasn't taking to the Executive Success Program teachings in the way I'd hoped. Instead, she was skeptical of a few of the practices that Nancy was teaching and didn't like the rules or rituals. I noticed she never recited the mission statement at the start of each day, and she fell asleep a couple times in class. In ESP terms, Mom was "disintegrated" and unwilling to pay tribute to what ESP had built. Despite that, Nancy either moved on with the material unfazed or giggled away my mom's comments and tried to convince me she simply thought my mother was charming. Mom quieted down but gave me a side-eye that spoke a thousand words—her unobtrusive way of making it clear that she would respect my choices but was not fully OK with this. *Oh, Mom*, I thought. Having an only child had always made her a little extra protective and involved when it came to my life. "I think your mom might have a tough time fully embracing the tech," one of the coaches told me in private. "Sometimes therapists have to choose between this thinking and their own training."

My mom and I had arranged to stay separately from each other, at the homes of two different Espians. Over lunch at a restaurant, she asked me, "Are you interested in other modalities too?" At this point, no, I wasn't. I wanted to climb the Stripe Path.

If her own questions about ESP had influenced me at all during this trip, that fell away at the end of this Five-Day. Because I had enrolled my mom, David, and my pal Nicki, the coaches awarded me with another red stripe on my white sash—and that wasn't all. Before we left to go home, the senior levels also held a small ceremony where they promoted me from a white sash to a yellow sash . . . which meant I was now what they considered an "apprentice coach." The promotion came from Dawn Morrison, a thin brunette who, as one of the women closest to Keith, had reached the highest training level and had one of the only twelve green sashes to show for it. I became conscious of my excitement—I was having a viscera!—when Dawn stood before the group to deliver a few words of praise about my progress over the past few months. She applauded my commitment to ESP and my drive in bringing them this handful of new enrollees from western Canada. I was bursting with pride as I bowed my head so Dawn could place the yellow sash around my neck. "Welcome to the rank of coach with all of the rights, responsibilities, and privileges that it entails," she said, shaking my hand with hers over mine.

Maybe it was foolish, but at the time I felt like witnessing my promotion from white sash to yellow would help to reassure my mother. I held back my grin as Mom sat quietly. Even a decade and a half later, the interaction between the two of us is palpable to me: me, feeling thrilled for my progress while not wanting to disappoint her; Mom, harboring concern while recognizing my happiness and not wanting to limit me. Looking back and now as a mother myself, I can imagine she must have felt like she was watching her daughter accept a marriage proposal from a dishonorable partner—except NXIVM as an organization was so much more powerful than any one person. At that stage, my mother's fear was that I was being sucked into a black hole of coercion and lies. "Just be careful," she said. "I don't think any one person can be credited with having all the answers."

But she was forgetting: Keith Raniere was known to be one of the smartest men in the world. "Who says that about themselves? Only a megalomaniac," she said under her breath. I ignored her. I was on my way in NXIVM. Now that they'd made me a yellow sash, this would be like an unpaid internship, but now I could attend intensives for free. I'd also be shadowing the highly skilled trainers, which, I was told, would help me move up the Stripe Path quickly to reach proctor status as a full, legitimate coach. When the upper levels determined you were ready to become a proctor, then you could officially start on one of the career paths within the company and finally get paid for all the time you put in.

My relationship with my mom wasn't the only place where certain things weren't being said. Not long after our trip to Albany, I couldn't help feeling there was something Nicki was holding back when she revealed to me that she was thinking about moving to NXIVM's home base. "Wait," I said. "You're *moving* to Albany?"

Yeah, she answered sheepishly. Apparently Keith had said he was going to help her with some of her acting "and stuff."

She'd been in for less than a year. How long had she been thinking about this? In a way, I was even a little jealous: why had Keith invited her to move to Albany, but not me? I had just gotten promoted to yellow. His team of executives agreed on my potential, but somehow he had overlooked me. Nicki hadn't even enrolled anybody yet.

I started to compare my growth against that of my peers. By now, Mark had advanced ahead of me. Nicki clearly also had the intention to make big moves. So it wasn't long after my second Five-Day that I made the decision to go for proctor, which would come with an orange sash. This was both a big decision and an obvious next step for someone for whom the program was really clicking. I'd been told that going from yellow to orange was like a "practical MBA," and that the skills I would learn were those a person would need to run a small company. From the time I was a kid, I'd sold crafts that I'd made and had always felt some passion to be an entrepreneur. I'd just never taken anything official that would grant me with proper business background.

When I informed the upper ranks of my intention, they expressed excitement that I was willing to come onboard. I was prepared to go through whatever kind of exam or certification process was required— but instead, they advised me that all I'd need to do was to get four stripes on my yellow sash.

In the few months since my Five-Day, I'd come to see the proctors as the ones in the program who had committed themselves to their growth, worked through their issues, and cultivated a mastery of their lives. To me, they had it figured out. They exuded confidence; a proctor was the point person who could offer advice and authority to a lower-level rank who needed some support and direction. There was an assumption that a proctor could see things that the lower ranks simply could not.

Nancy told me it was possible for me to reach proctor status in as little as three to six months and that one of the main criteria for promotion to proctor was to have enrolled seventeen people in your "organization," and that at least two had to be earning their way up the Stripe Path. Nicki Clyne was already doing that, and David had started the Stripe Path not far behind her.

I would receive my training from Barbara Bouchey, who was highly skilled at the sales tactics that Keith pushed so hard. Simply put, I'd be learning from the best. To learn the tech, I would have to shadow-coach as many intensives as it would take to grasp the inductive reasoning that the organization called Rational Inquiry, which Keith called a "human technology . . . that we apply to different situations to get certain types of results."

This system of educating a new ESP student allowed space for our trainers to guide our thoughts and behaviors so as to make our beliefs consistent with our actions. The inductive component was that Rational Inquiry was designed to be experiential so that we would come to conclusions on our own, which is why the breakthroughs seemed so powerful. While other workshops had people at the front of the room giving us information, ESP was a process that was supposed to create perceptual shifts. This would make the awareness permanent and life-changing. Getting to proctor meant learning to give EMs, using Rational Inquiry, learning to coach the entire Sixteen-Day, and evolving your issues.

But it was very systematic—what cult experts call a "closed-loop system of logic." ESP contended that the way you live and view the world comes through the filters of your experience. So while this process of inductive reasoning appeared to have been designed to empower us, it also left room for us to be set up for manipulation. For example, the main question in Rational Inquiry was "What do you mean?" or "What do you make it mean?" If someone were to have a reaction about Keith doing anything that could be considered "wrong," a coach could turn it around on that individual by asking: "What do you make it mean? What's bad about it?" Any reaction can be spun as one's own issue.

I attended as many trainings as they offered and in just a few months I'd also enrolled close to a dozen family and friends. Barbara Bouchey told me that for a lot of people, the trickiest part for a yellow sash to rise to orange is to work out his or her emotional issues. There were several components to the process to track my progress and hold me accountable. First, I undertook a weekly one-hour session the company called Goals Lab, phone calls or Skype sessions where I'd check in with my goals coach to discuss whether I was overcoming my limitations in order to progress successfully toward my aim of getting my orange sash, and discuss next steps. I studied to show them my proficiency in the principles, the curriculum, and the sales techniques.

I flew myself to every Five-Day they offered, including one in Monterey, Mexico, and now I was playing a small role in helping to run the intensives. At the end of each one, I received the next red stripe on my yellow sash. I had reached the next level after proving I could run breakout groups and engage in deep rapport with individuals and with the group as a whole. Every stripe measured these interpersonal skills, and there was no stopping me.

At the end of six months, I still was not a proctor. The senior levels told me that I was a great coach, and I had long ago proven my enrollment skills. But enrollment wasn't what was holding me back from becoming a proctor. By now, I was way beyond the seventeen people I needed to enroll to earn my orange sash; plus I had enrolled almost three hundred people myself or through the students I'd personally brought in. Clare Bronfman had recently been promoted, and I didn't find her very warm or caring as a coach. Certainly it couldn't have been because of her money that she was growing, right? I couldn't fathom that. I believed promotions on the Stripe Path were purely merit-based.

I felt like no matter how many EMs I did or how many integrations I had—or, come on, how many friends and friends-of-friends I was enrolling—the higher-ups kept reminding me of my two core issues: control and my "like-me disease." Control. The need to be liked. OK. I'd keep working on those. Still, neither Barbara Bouchey nor Mark was able to give me a sense of when I would finally receive my orange proctor sash.

These were the same deficiencies that had come up for me in the Eleven-Day. The upper ranks kept reminding me of those and I'd keep beating myself up about them. *What else can I do?* Like a lot of people in the program, I'd begun to carry around what we called a "stimulus-response journal." The minute an event or interaction would trigger a reaction in me, I'd hurry and make note of it so that I could try to work it through in an EM later. *Every time someone does X*, I'd write, *I feel Y*. The EMs and the homework were taking up so much of my time, and by now I was so hyperaware of my reaction patterns that sometimes the practice felt more like a flogging than a tool for informing or empowering myself. Coming up on the two-year mark of working toward my orange sash, I sometimes longed for the days when I'd just walked through life reacting to things without itemizing every time I did.

Still, I was focused on my goal. I had put in so much time and I wasn't going to quit. I took my coaches' suggestions anytime a situation came up that threatened to send me spiraling into my old patterns. I implemented their emotional strategies and came back to each weekly Goals Lab with one of my coaches to share how that tool had worked. After two years going back and forth to Albany while I remained at yellow, for sure they'd promote me to orange, wouldn't they? But still, after my coach discussed it with Nancy and the upper ranks, we'd get onto our call the next week and they'd tell me I needed to keep working on myself. "Thank you for the feedback," I'd say, responding to their criticism of me in the way we'd been taught. If I'd have responded by saying "But—!" or "Would you at least agree I'm making some progress?" I knew there was a very real chance that my coaches would enforce Keith and Nancy's policy on someone who was acting entitled or mad-dogging a coach: I'd have to work EMs on these two issues alone for at least another year.

This was another hint I'd missed: discussing my progress was a one-way street. If you questioned the feedback, you were being "defensive." A higher-ranking coach once told me, "I'm experiencing you as being angry."

"I don't feel angry at all," I said. "What am I doing that would make you think that?"

"All feedback is valid," chimed in Lauren, and if we got defensive, that was feedback too, because it points to an "issue." I felt so cornered. There was no way out except to accept it. And then, ironically, I *was* angry.

But I was still determined to address my issues.

This was how I began to notice the other side of being "at-cause." Being willing to take ownership of what takes place in our lives and committing to that understanding can be empowering. But this awareness can also be used against you. Over the past few months but even as long ago as V-Week, when we'd observed Keith and the way he related to his upper ranks and the Espians, I had learned that if I had any inclination to express a concern about the program, a higher rank could simply say that it was my own issue. If I was being reactive, then I was "out of cause" and would need to work the issue and figure out why the given situation bothered me.

After almost three years of working on my issues in my efforts to reach orange, I could not think of another possible way I could address my control and dependence issues, and I was getting confused. When Keith asked us salespeople to fill a new program he'd just launched and I asked about the content and details, I received feedback that I was being controlling. My issue was being used against me for what I thought was my willingness to ask a question to be more effective in my role.

That's part of why I stayed quiet when I returned to Albany to attend another training that I hoped would help me advance. It had been a good year since Nicki Clyne and I had really talked. I reached out to her to see if we could get together since in our coaching sessions, she seemed to be "suffering"—ESP's term to describe someone who appeared to be miserable or overwhelmed. I thought maybe I could help her with her growth and enrollments toward getting to proctor. But when I called her, Nicki said that she couldn't meet up with me because she had to be available for Keith.

Available? I thought. Her use of the word struck me as strange.

Are they sleeping together?

No way. She's in her early twenties. He's fifty-something. In a flash of question, I asked myself if something sexual was happening. I believed there was no way Keith would do something like that, especially with a young, innocent woman who'd just moved 2,500 miles in the hopes of building her career.

The way Nicki had abandoned her life in Canada and now seemed like a stranger to me felt like a loss, but more than anything I didn't want to push her even further away. I had asked her at one point about her acting career, but she brushed the question aside in an almost holier-than-thou response about how acting was irrelevant compared with the values she was upholding by representing ESP out in the world. I felt judged and somewhat ashamed of my acting goals, and I wouldn't feel close to her anymore from this point.

Either way, she chose to come here, and Keith was her mentor. *It would be totally inappropriate for someone in a therapeutic role to start a sexual relationship with someone in the "patient" or "client" role. It would break every ethical guideline.* I dismissed my intuition because I just didn't think it was possible! Keith, as we had been told from day one, was a celibate renunciate.

So I continued to work those EMs in order to get my orange sash. Ever since I got my coach sash, I had been attending classes down at the Tacoma center. I had established a new routine each weekend: on Saturday morning, I would leave before the sun came up to drive five hours and cross the U.S. border into Washington State. In Tacoma, I'd take three classes from 10 A.M. till 6 P.M. Then I'd drive back to Vancouver so I didn't have to pay for a hotel room, slipping quietly into the apartment around midnight and walking on tiptoe so as not to wake David. This happened almost every weekend for months. I wanted to show them that I was committed to my growth and would become a proctor so that I could open an Ethos center in Vancouver.

"People always say they're going to bring ESP to their country," Nancy had told me when we first met, "but they're rarely committed enough to follow through on that."

"For real," I said. "I'm going to do it." I would show them I could keep advancing on the Stripe Path and prove my commitment to myself and the organization.

Perhaps the strongest motivation for me was the first time I led a student to an epiphany in understanding her old pattern in an intensive. It was one of the first Five-Days I coached in Tacoma and when I asked her just the right inductive question, she had a massive awareness as she integrated and broke down crying. It hit me: this was an even sweeter, more powerful moment than experiencing an integration for myself. It was also the very same reason I'd gotten into acting: to lead people to experience an emotional impact that would move them to make permanent shifts. It was so satisfying, and it felt like I was catching on naturally to this methodology.

I've come to call this first chunk of time in ESP "the intern years," the period of time when I was paying my dues to break in and establish myself. With my acting money and the 20 percent commission I earned on the friends I had enrolled, I was able to pay for the higher-level trainings I needed to keep advancing. I had started offering Five-Day trainings in Vancouver, but I wasn't getting paid for them. Those fourteen-hour days were part of what NXIVM considered the "ethical value exchange," which was essentially the same kind of work exchange David and I had participated in when we supported Mark's filming of V-Week. Still, the senior-level coaches reminded me, I was earning my way toward that "practical MBA" they'd referred to when I'd put myself on the path toward proctor. Sold on this dream, I stuck with it. Working to build the Vancouver community would keep me challenged and motivated.

Not only did I buy into the "exchange concept," I loved it. Each week I rented two hours' worth of office space at a shared workspace in the Gastown neighborhood. Various coaches would help me set up and tear down, carrying all of the notes, iPods, sashes, and materials every time we were teaching. Even with all the grunt work and investment, this was a blast. Mark would fly in to do an intro presentation, and it was my job per NXIVM practice to "edify" him—to talk him up for the audience of forty or fifty of my friends and *their* friends, loosening them up to help get them excited about what was coming. "Have you guys seen *What the Bleep Do We Know!?*" I was aware that I was piggybacking on Mark's success as several heads around the room nodded. "If you liked that film," I'd continue, "then you'll love this. Not only is the director of *What the Bleep!?* about to enlighten you, but we're all going to have a ton of fun." And we did. After a minute, one of my friends might answer an ice-breaker question that I'd pose, or a student in the back might interject some tongue-in-cheek comment that would get everybody laughing.

Then Mark would transition into the intro while I stood back to absorb this audience, trying to guess who would sign up. Most Vancouverites would probably agree that our city has always been full of conscious, educated individuals—people who love hikes, healthy eating, and spiritual practice. The people we were enrolling in their twenties and thirties were all coming by word-of-mouth and were like sponges for this information. At each session, faces from the week before would reappear with a friend or two at their side. Enrollment was increasing exponentially. Reporting our attendance numbers into Albany each week was getting more and more electrifying.

"What'd you think?" I'd ask the crowd in Prefect's style to debrief at the end of an intensive.

"I don't know if I really understand what this is all about . . ." someone would say, "but I like the vibe of the community." At the Vancouver center, they weren't always coming for the content. They were coming for the people.

In terms of sales, I was making that work. With Barbara Bouchey, I had worked enough EMs to get over my earlier hang-ups about accepting other people's money. With hundreds of Vancouver people finding our teachings, I understood what Barbara had meant when she'd explained that we were offering an invaluable service. I didn't see the financial ask as a motive anymore; it was just a piece of the enroll-ment process. I'd gotten the hang of a particular sales approach that Keith called a "lift." This was the strategy that helped just about any new enrollee overcome their early hesitation to spend their money on ESP. You had to build multiple lifts, kind of like climbing a staircase from one step to another, to get them to the point where $2,000 for a workshop was a no-brainer.

There were three main lifts to achieve that goal. First you'd start with a strategy that the company called "rapport." Basically, you needed to hit it off with any individual and establish to them that you were trustworthy and relatable. "How are you doing today, are you enjoying the weather outside?" "I love that top you're wearing; it was the first thing I noticed when you walked in!" It wasn't disin-genuous; in fact, I had always connected easily to others . . . and to the leaders of NXIVM, that attribute of my personality translated to added value.

The second step of a lift was for me, the salesperson, to identify the individual's need. After we'd established that degree of rapport, I was trained to lead the discussion smoothly to pin down why the newcomer had shown up in the first place. "This may or may not be for you," I might say, "but why are you here? What are you seeking?" Their answer would become the leash I'd use to guide their partici-pation from that point. Some were looking for a long-term romantic partner. Some wanted greater career success. Others simply wanted to surround themselves with a community of peers who also had big goals in life. I didn't pounce; I listened with authenticity. This program had given me the support I'd needed to keep on the path toward my goals, I shared with a prospective student. My angle to approach this was different from the way Barbara Bouchey, who'd made a career as a finance professional, had scolded me about money right before I'd enrolled—but the goal was the same. After all, they *needed* this mate-rial. And then, we made it possible.

Because the third step was to get them to agree that they couldn't accomplish this on their own. "Wouldn't you agree it would be worth three thousand dollars if you could make more money/have your dream career/procrastinate less?" I'd ask them. Still receptive to my unassuming disposition, most prospective enrollees would shrug and answer, *Yeah.* "Well, good!" I'd say. "Then let's find the money." From there it was a short process of putting our heads together, sometimes along with one or two of our senior coaches, to help this person obtain the finances or arrange for a work exchange like the one that made it possible for David and me to attend V-Week. NXIVM's slogan for step three of the lift was: "Turn *if* into *how.*"

But the end game wasn't even in getting that yes. The true goal was to home in on an individual's need. That need had the shining potential to become the company's wealth. Not that I could see it that way at the time. My base assumption was the foundation of what I believed: that we were doing something positive in the world. Our work was helping people break through their limitations and have the life they wanted. Each new prospective enrollee couldn't see that they were just a pawn being moved across a chessboard by Keith and Nancy. Nor could I. To me, building trust with someone new was everything. To our founders, building trust was just a ploy. In fact, the entire company was leveraging trust—a term I learned later when I was ready to dismantle my sales training and cult indoctrination.

A stranger's revelation of what they hoped to get from ESP was a salesperson's powerful "in" with a new enrollee. My job as a salesperson was to elicit their dreams—that was the entry point. I wasn't overbearing in the way I'd noticed Nancy Salzman could be; I wasn't socially awkward like some of the more senior instructors (whose actual coaching skills were admirable). From the sincerest and most heartfelt place, it was easy for me to get along with new enrollees and make our new students feel comfortable.

I also trusted that anyone who took a training would get value for their money, especially when I paid Lauren to fly out to Vancouver to train a group. Because of Lauren's familiarity with the material as NXIVM's head of education, she was a fun and engaging instructor and always popular among my friends, acquaintances, and new recruits. Lauren wasn't a field trainer whose job was to focus on sales. She was more like Keith and Nancy—one of the program developers, one of the visionaries, and her opinions held a lot of weight. She clearly had a lot of authority within NXIVM. She usually stayed at a hotel not far from my apartment, and we would meet up and spend the day together before the Five-Day started. It was a blossoming friendship as much as it was a business partnership. Lauren's time in Vancouver allowed her to evaluate me so that I could advance in the company, while simultaneously giving the company a chance to grow into Canada. This was beneficial for all of us—we were evolving consciousness throughout the world.

By now, David and I had used our Goals Lab to move out of the basement apartment and buy a bigger place together. Now, on some mornings when she flew to Vancouver, Lauren came over while I prepared breakfast—oatmeal with nuts and berries, eggs with avocado and spinach—before we took long walks by the ocean near my apartment. We went shopping and for pedicures, where the nail techs served us tea as Lauren and I talked about her journey in ESP. I asked her about her experience in reaching green-sash status, but mostly we discussed the team in Vancouver that I was building. She advised me on how to grow my coaches and shared her opinion on what certain enrollees might be struggling with as they journeyed up the Stripe Path. She was so smart and bubbly, always with great suggestions and solutions. I appreciated that she cared enough to think critically about the experiences of the people from our center. I knew her mom expected us to recruit at turbospeed, but Lauren genuinely cared about the new enrollees.

Sometimes after trainings Lauren would stay an extra day or two to train our staff in the tech or teach us how to run the exercises that were part of the Eleven-Day. It was a huge privilege to have her time as we congregated with a sincere intention to grow and become more skilled at helping others. Lauren approved the moves I was making as we held forty-person trainings and tried to grow the community, with the goal of reaching enough attendees that we could open an actual center. A year and a half into my work in ESP, the TV series *Smallville* was filming in Vancouver. Allison Mack, a young actress who played one of the leads on the show, came to an early Jness intensive with one of her co-stars when Lauren approached her and began showering her with attention. They both seemed so fake, and I felt really jealous as they carried on saying things like, "Wait, *you* like knitting? I like knitting! We should totally knit together!"

Allison was on hiatus from filming and although she'd just met Lauren, she decided to fly out to Albany with her the following morning. They left together and I tore down the intensive feeling forgotten . . . left out. I thought back to the first time I met Lauren, and then to how she had acted with Allison the night before. I was the one building this center and attracting these cool young professionals. It really hurt that Lauren could so easily jump to a new best friend.

In part, the increasingly strategic interpersonal relationships in the community pushed me to prove myself in spite of an unrealistic business model. If you wanted to open a center, you needed one hundred paying students. Until that point, all the students who were signing up in Vancouver had to trek down to the Tacoma center for most of their trainings beyond the Five-Day. I as the coach wasn't entitled to any additional payment beyond the commission for my direct enrollees, and I'd been paying out of pocket to rent the space. Once you finally hit one hundred members, you received only 10 percent commission for everyone who enrolled at your center *in addition* to the 20 percent you earned for your direct enrollees. In my case, because friends like Nicki Clyne and several others were all enrolled through my center, they were considered to be within my lineage. The executives called it a "onesie-twosie" when one of your enrollees enrolled another student, and the lineage was casually (and lovingly) known as our "duckies." To receive 20 percent commission each time your own friend enrolled in something new *plus* only 10 percent of the enrollment cost from anyone they brought in—this might sound pretty lucrative. Actually, it wasn't even enough to rent a facility that would house the center.

I guess I was running on the sheer fumes of optimism that if I showed enough commitment and delivered enough new students to them, then certainly at some point they would decide to promote me to orange. Those first few years, I worked for free, coached for free, and made some money on commissions when I referred people to the

Five-Day. I had learned the sales technique, and man, I was grinding to bring newbies in. I called on my coachees often, and, as Nancy had once said, some of the group from the Vancouver center had become like family—in fact, for a lot of people the connections they made in the Executive Success Program replaced their actual familial relationships. It's a tactic called "love bombing" and is characteristic of many cults: to tell someone who's seeking genuine connection with others that they're "like family" is a manipulative way to make them feel they've finally found the place where they belong.

This extremely close atmosphere became a big part of what kept me going when, after a couple of years at the level of yellow, they still had not given me my orange sash. I learned that despite what they'd suggested to me about the possibility that I could reach it in six months, only one person in the history of the organization had ever done so. That was Alex Betancourt, who was close friends with some of the most powerful figures at the Mexico City centers for the company. At this point I was more focused on growing the Vancouver community than I was my own advancement. I got permission to run Ethos modules once a week in downtown Vancouver. This way, the Vancouver students wouldn't have to make the epic journey to Tacoma for Ethos classes.

No, I wasn't getting paid regularly, but it was a welcome supplement to my income from acting. And while most of the money I was making went back into the business, I was able to put that out of my mind. I was coaching others and leading seminars to help build an organization that was changing the world. Of course it would take extraordinary commitment and sacrifices!

Wouldn't it?

I was trying not to be disillusioned. Mark Vicente had joined NXIVM right before I had, but he'd already advanced beyond yellow and orange and was on the brink of being promoted to green, meaning he'd soon gain permission to run his own center. But in order for him to be rewarded with a green sash, the company required that one of his direct enrollments be promoted from yellow to orange. No yellow sash under Mark was better positioned for this than I was . . . and for three years now, that's what I'd been working toward.

And because my main goal was to open an actual center, I needed that proctor status too. At this time we were also supposed to be proficient at EMs, so I did hundreds of EM "drills" to get better and took tech classes from Lauren. Next to Nancy, there was no one better at these than Lauren.

Today, I look back and see my error clearly. No person should ever work without a guaranteed salary or with only the "promise" that one day, they *might* gain employment at the organization they're training with. In legitimate corporations, employees don't pay their own money to receive training unless it's for some type of continuing education or a real shot at promotion. Chasing money with more money in hopes of getting promoted was such a huge mistake.

But with dreams of eventually opening the Vancouver center, I continued to pump all my earnings back into the company.

Lauren was my favorite teacher, and in those earliest days of devotion I planned a trip to meet her in Miami, where I'd help her with a Five-Day. "Maybe we can stay together," I said.

"Oh," she replied, "I'd rather have my own room." She rolled in two huge suitcases, in which she'd packed five different pairs of black flip-flops. *And I have control issues, they say . . .?* I wound up rooming with another coach, and we had a great time—but I would've loved to have had that with Lauren.

When I felt discouraged or left out about not being promoted or included, I reminded myself of the real reason I was doing this. Within the ESP community in Vancouver, we were helping each other grow and work through limitations. I felt so purposeful and motivated from that. I couldn't give up. If I did, the whole community in Vancouver would fall apart. All the love I'd put into building the center I wanted to open and getting my orange sash had brought me so close. I was determined to prove myself to Keith, Nancy, and my peers . . . and most of all, to myself.

PART TWO

THE GOLDEN YEARS

2009–2012

CHAPTER SIX

PERSISTENCY

2009

He thought Holly was hotter.

Around 2008 at a training David and I attended in Albany, we'd engaged in an exercise called Rating & Ranking. We broke into small groups for a practice that was supposed to illustrate for us how we perceive others based on their physical appearance and other nonverbal characteristics. But like so many pieces of the tech over the years, instead of empowering us with wisdom and insight, this could really damage some people.

In this particular exercise, our job was to rank each person in our group in the following categories based on our perception of them; by doing this we'd become more conscious of how we interact with people based on what we think of them. The categories were: Who was the smartest? Who was the most honest? Who was the most sexually attractive? You had to rate your own attributes compared with others, and then you had to read your responses aloud to your group. The practice was painful in exposing how we compared ourselves against others, and even more hurtful in what it revealed when it was time for everyone to announce how they'd ranked one another.

In this round, of course I rated David as the male I found the most sexually attractive—he was sitting right there in my group, and even if one of the guys had been more striking physically, David and I had been together for three years and built a lot of trust and intimacy.

Sexual attraction wasn't just about who's the best-looking. Without question, I found him the sexiest. I loved him. He was my partner.

But when David's turn came to share his ranked results, he announced to our group that he'd rated Holly, the pretty blonde, as the most sexually attractive.

My insides dropped. I'd thought my boyfriend would be sensitive enough not to hurt me. Trying to pull myself out of the fog this had caused in my mind, I thought I heard David say something like, *We were supposed to be honest here, right?* As Holly and the entire discussion group examined me awkwardly, I tried to take it gracefully, as if I'd just received news that another actress had been chosen for a part I'd really wanted. Maintaining porcelain composure and hoping to change the subject, I carefully slid my glasses onto my face. With this alteration to my appearance, in the next round of the exercise later in the day a few of them changed their rankings, rating me as the most intelligent. To me, it felt like an act of pity.

To be fair, David had been too solid a guy for me to end our long-term relationship over something this silly. When we wound up splitting at around this time, it was because of a larger issue between us that ESP had brought to the surface. "You two don't really share the same values anymore," my coach observed. This was the senior levels' standard diagnosis when someone in a couple was moving faster up the Stripe Path than the other. In cases like this for heterosexual couples, I noticed that the faster-rising member was almost always the woman. "You're constantly on the phone, coaching people," David had complained. I couldn't disagree. Even as I peed and brushed my teeth before bed, I was on the phone with new recruits, students, and coachees to help them with their goals and struggles.

As soon as I ended the relationship, my position in the company changed. I began to travel to Albany at least once a quarter, where each day I was interacting with the highest senior executives—mostly Lauren, with whom I'd grown very close over the past four years. When I traveled to Albany for a training, I still rented private rooms at the homes of other Espians, even though I sought more quality time with Lauren. It seemed she was always on the go to check on her cats or run an errand for Keith. If we spent time together, it was usually while we scarfed down a bagged lunch during a break in a training and then used the rest of the time to take a walk outside. Everyone in Albany was vegetarian, and anytime we had a potluck, there was zero meat allowed—because, as the senior levels had preached to me and as I had begun to instill in others, "Keith does not believe in violence." I'd learned to try to honor Lauren's food choices but at times I was a little concerned. While it seemed like the women in Albany were always on some kind of fast, trying methods like juicing, raw foods, and a liquids-only diet, Lauren sometimes made choices that gave her even less nourishment: a few packs of saltine crackers and apple juice—that was it, all day—or a couple of pieces of candy. "My hair," she'd sometimes groan, and it was obvious to me that it was thinning. Albany wasn't a city flush with health food stores, but I often suggested we go out for a green smoothie to try to encourage Lauren to get some vitamins and nutrients. She'd agree with a sneaky smile, as if we were getting away with something by treating ourselves to a smoothie with nut butter or avocado blended in.

As I think about it now, I'd say there were times when I had the feeling that my presence gave my friend a break, a fingertip's touch to the outside world. I believe she lived a life of such strict personal discipline that she felt the need to be punished for even the most normal kindness she showed herself. To think that even nourishing her body seemed like a treat made me sad for her. What Keith and her mother had developed was a system framed in large part around what I've since learned, that controlling food intake is a common practice in many cults. In particular, restricting intake of protein and/or sugar leaves participants in a literal brain haze. I didn't see it nearly this clearly back then, but I was aware that there were moments when I felt a longing to try to help her. Even in old photos together, our arms are wrapped around each other while her smile often appears forced, straining to accept my unbridled love for her . . . my best friend.

The ways we all related to each other had various unspoken parameters and expectations. As I spent more time at the homes of the senior leaders based in Albany, I noticed that most of them had chosen to furnish their living spaces with sectional sofas, offering plenty of seating for groups to gather for meetings there. Lauren and I would sometimes congregate with the other leaders in Nancy's living room, where Lauren would curl up with her cat, Mimi, a hairless Siamese. Her fashion and decor always seemed very intentional although her aim was for it all to appear effortless—a style that Keith took to characterizing as "boho-chic girly meets bag lady," a label that I'd once noticed made Lauren drop her gaze in what I thought was a reaction of embarrassment. He had a way of dishing out insults in front of an audience, always under the guise of teaching someone and helping them with their issue. It never felt good to watch, and you never wanted to be the recipient. Lauren was so loyal to Keith, but she was often the subject of his put-downs.

In our opportunities to have quiet time together, Lauren and I chatted about the normal things young women talk about: work and our careers, the blogs or books we were reading, new TV shows we were watching, whatever fitness routine we were into. Health and nutrition remained the only areas where I felt like an authority, as I urged her to take more vitamins and buy protein powder, to nourish herself with supplements because I continued to fear that her diet was far too restrictive. I sometimes noted that what didn't come up often was the topic most women spend hours dishing on together: guys. Lauren was a year older than I was and didn't date, it appeared . . . and somewhere in the recesses of my mind, I registered a conscious thought: *why had all the women in this program made NXIVM the center of their lives?* Few of the senior executives or field trainers were married or in any kind of committed partnership—in fact, I knew a few who had left long-term relationships once they'd really gotten on a roll with their careers in the company.

I wondered if this way of life had been so meaningful to them that they'd become fully willing to give up relationships; or whether, in a less constructive way, it simply consumed so much of their focus that they didn't have time to meet new people who might be relationship material. Or, even worse (and I'd have never asked this question out loud), whether this material was so off-the-wall that a potential partner just wouldn't get it. It was awesome and so reassuring to be surrounded by this tight-knit community. But might it be a little too insular?

As I became closer to the community, I also had to wonder: was this solo way of life what they intended for me, too? I had always wanted a husband and children, and I was afraid that my coaches would frown on that, or even hold me back from being promoted if I wasn't willing to give up my dreams of wanting a family. I'd been willing to submit to the organization's principles in every other aspect of my life, and I feared that this one desire, which I held more strongly than any other, would be the thing that even in this place where they *said* I belonged would make it impossible for me to ever *really* belong. In our trainings, we'd been taught that things from the outside world—including relationships and love—were just noninte-grated fixations. I knew it was likely they believed that my need for a relationship made me "dependent," but I hoped to eventually build a connection with someone who shared my values. Someone in the company who would not just "fill the deficiency" but would grow with me. I was independent and was even in the process of looking to buy an apartment in Vancouver on my own. There was a private part of me that felt shame and concern about my future with NXIVM for wanting both a career with this company *and* a life partner and kids. For now, there was no urgency. I was newly single, and our community was growing. For all I knew, I could meet an amazing guy at a training in Los Angeles or Mexico. I would allow myself some space just to focus on my work and keep these questions about my future to myself.

I was a little comforted to find that on some level, Lauren had also struggled with this. She hinted to me at one point that she had a little something going on with a guy within the organization. "Come on!" I teased her. "Tell me who!" But she remained tight-lipped in a way that made me cognizant that my friend had a really hard time letting people in. I was so flattered the first time I heard her refer to me as her *best* friend—I valued that she thought so highly of me as a person and a professional. But it kind of bugged me: what girl doesn't share the details of her romantic life with her *best friend*? David had remained active in Vancouver's Ethos program after our breakup, and I shared with Lauren every detail of what it was like to be friends with my ex. It wasn't easy, but I was pretty impressed by our mutual commitment to making it work. Sometimes, even when we weren't in coaching mode, I couldn't understand why Lauren kept me at arm's length. I've always been really open about my experiences and feelings, and the way she held her emotions so close to the vest made me wonder what she really thought of me whenever I opened up to her.

Visiting Albany at least once a quarter made me privy to inside news, and things were getting interesting. Allison Mack and I had actually grown closer, and when I was in Albany we'd grab lunch together during a break from training or go for a walk. I was her upline proctor, trying to work with her on recruiting. It wasn't one of her strengths, and she often just paid people's fees on their behalf to get them to commit to a training.

Through some of the Vancouver actresses and other connections, we expanded even deeper into Hollywood. "You're like family!" I would sometimes overhear Nancy tell our high-profile new enrollees. It irked me. Was everyone who'd ever worked in front of a camera "like family" to her?

But—*if* we were like family, then these were good connections to have. We were gaining traction with so many celebrities that Mark was aggressively focusing on growing the Los Angeles Ethos community. Clare and Sara Bronfman, the daughters of the billionaire Edgar Bronfman Sr., were becoming more involved. Later they would buy an island in Fiji—fucking *Fiji*—that the company would use, and on their farmland outside Albany they held massive parties complete with white tents and entertainment. Both sisters were placid, if . . . different. Sara, with the blonder curly hair, was the more self-aware of the two; Clare appeared more physically delicate but, frankly, I found her less friendly. Both had mild British accents from the years they'd spent at boarding school in the UK, and from what I'd picked up on they both had kind of a tumultuous relationship with their dad. I was so excited that Allison Mack and some of the other young women in my lineage had made plans to come on a field trip I'd arranged for us to see the Dalai Lama, since Sara Bronfman was close with one of his advisors. But when we arrived, Allison and Sara took off on a designer shopping spree. They'd determined between the two of them that I couldn't afford to join them.

Few of us were close with the Bronfmans. Around this time when I attended a new sales training at Nancy's house in the Albany suburbs with a group of about a dozen, I noticed how every time Clare raised her hand to ask a question about the sales technique, she lavished Keith in tribute in a way that made it apparent to me that she was deeply enamored with him. He nodded languidly as she praised his genius, as if to say, *Yes, yes, you're right. I am that brilliant. Well done for noticing.* It was forbidden for us ever to gossip or talk about other members of the team, so I resisted the urge to try to catch Lauren's eye, observing instead as she bit the inside of her cheek in silence.

My commitment to the company had helped me to overcome my former tendency to be a quitter when things got challenging. Also, practicing Keith's philosophy of "persistency," or a full commitment to a practice on a daily basis, had become a natural part of my approach to getting anything done and changing my behavior. The idea was that you would commit to practicing a skill or new habit—like learning Spanish or exercising—for a minimum of thirty days (a practice that I would later find to be taught in multiple other self-help books and seminars). I had had multiple "persistencies" over the years, but now I was working on my sales skills so I could learn to do the intro presentations myself and not rely on Mark Vicente. One day, around this time, we were called out of the blue to fly to Albany for a training where all of the field trainers would have the great privilege to learn a new "intro" from Keith himself. He'd begun to coach us on how to sound more convincing in our presentations by choosing dramatic gestures and using certain intonations and long pauses. Several of my peers stepped before the group one at a time and echoed the script we'd been developing and learning all weekend. "Are we going to have fun?" they'd start, as we'd been taught, and then they'd jump into the pitch. Keith gave each of the other salespeople a sentence or two of critique, or else something along the lines of "Decent, have a seat." But when he called me to take the floor, the procedure was totally different.

"Are we going to have fun?" I asked the group.

Keith cut me off immediately, like an impatient director on set. "Are we gonna have fun? Are we gonna have *fun*?" Nancy recently had made a project of working on Keith's personal style. He'd cut his hair from biblical to collar-length, more like somebody who had a real full-time job in an office. He'd also traded in his outdated square-rimmed glasses for a rounder frame, reminiscent of Steve Jobs—and instead of the golf shirts I'd seen him wear that sometimes bore wet marks around the underarms, he'd taken to wearing cashmere V-neck sweaters, often with a gleaming white T-shirt underneath. For the first time, he actually looked the part of someone who led a company. "Come on!" he chided me. "Tell us: we're gonna have *fun*!"

I felt sweat break out across my upper lip but was unable to anticipate what was coming for the next half hour. Keith made an example of me in front of my friends and the upper ranks, having me repeat the new script like a drill sergeant. I was the only professional actor in the room that day, but his ridicule of my delivery made me feel as though I was the only one who was under this much scrutiny, being tested this way, and the only one who hadn't mastered the new intro format. I felt incredibly self-conscious. With me still standing in front of the group, he pulled out a deck of cards and used me like a magician's assistant so he could perform a card trick. "OK," he said, as if he was cutting me a break. "Come here. Pick a card." I paused for a moment and finally stepped toward him to pull one card gently from the deck. After a few rounds of successfully guessing what card I'd selected from the stack, he revealed to the group that he was able to tell which card I'd chosen simply by the way I was holding it in my hand.

"Pick another one. Do you trust me?"

I paused. "Yes?" In the video, the word comes out unconvincingly, as a quiet question. With his hand he'd gesture for me to come closer. Tentatively I'd take a step forward and choose another card, as if I feared a snake was going to jump out of a jack-in-the-box the second I got too close.

There was absolutely no context for the card trick, no point to it that I could see. Ten years later as I watch video of this entire interaction (because he insisted everything be taped), I can see how guarded I was. My arms were crossed in front of me; I hung back at a noticeable distance until again he would instruct me to come nearer to him. For a long time during this exchange, I stood leaning far back on one heel, as if subconsciously I wanted to move away without him noticing. The position of my lower body as I view the video shows me: even before I was aware of it, I had one foot in, and one foot out.

After close to an hour of this charade, he finally dismissed me to take my seat back on Nancy's sofa with my friends, while offering one of the only compliments he bestowed on me in my twelve years with the company. "Nice job," he said. My colleagues all looked on, as though wishing it had been them but also glad it hadn't. Having Keith's attention was something to be envied. "I can't believe you did that," a few whispered to me later. "I couldn't have done that in front of everybody. That was really brave."

I'd faced Keith, willing to fail in front of everybody.

Ten years later, I can see that this was his way of attempting to intimidate me into submission. It was the childish way a little boy in grade school calls a girl mean names, just to see if he can capture her attention. Nowadays, in NLP methods that pick-up artists use they call it "negging."

It was known that Keith loved to engage in physical activity with those closest to him in the organization, especially the women. In Albany he was known to play volleyball three times a week into the wee hours of the morning at a bleak sports barn called ABC Fitness. During these volleyball matches, or walking around the neighborhoods of Clifton Park with one or two other women, he would discuss life and philosophy and the development of the company.

Shortly after my breakup with David, when I was spending more time in Albany, Keith asked Mark to invite me to take a walk with him. I thought it was so strange that he sent someone to ask me to go with him, like the boys in junior high who would put one of their friends up to delivering a note to a girl—except I honestly didn't pick up on any romantic interest. "Why don't you spend more time with Keith?" Pam Cafritz would ask me. "Why don't you ask him to go for a walk?"

For a while he persisted with these invitations, always through a third party. "Sorry," I said later to Keith when we were face-to-face after a meeting. "I'm flying back to Vancouver in the morning for an audition; I just flew in and out this trip. I can't change my flight to go on a walk with you."

"You're leaving?" Keith asked me. "Already?"

"Yeah. I have to get back."

"What time's your flight?"

"8 A.M."

"I'm not free until 11."

In response I gave him a look that said, *Sorry, then I guess a walk's not happening.*

The other Espians would ask me: "You wouldn't change your flight to spend time with *Keith*?"

I was underwhelmed. "No."

Mark was invested in my growth and urged me to take advantage of these one-on-one meetings with Keith. One night before I was scheduled to fly out in the morning, he gave me a heads-up. "Keith might free up between 1 and 4 A.M. Keep your phone on." If we were expecting a call from Keith, we had to keep a voice recorder close by so that anything he said could either be archived in the library of wisdom he and Nancy kept, or so that we could remember everything as "class-one," firsthand data we could refer back to at any time.

I never slept with my ringer on, but this one time I would oblige—but so that I could fall asleep easily before my early flight, I'd taken melatonin at bedtime. When the phone rang in the dark hours of early morning, I fumbled for my phone and could hear myself slurring as Keith tried to talk me into staying so we could walk together the next morning.

That was his obedience test: *How willing are you to make yourself available to me?* I just wasn't. The next few times he sent someone to invite me on a walk with him, I turned it down because it conflicted with something I'd already scheduled.

"Keith meets effort with effort," Mark advised me. I responded with confused silence as I tried to work out what this meant . . . then

I got it: Keith required you to take a step to get closer to him before he would take a step to get closer with you. Mark told me that calling Keith more often and sending him emails would be a good way to get over whatever it was that was holding me back from being vulnerable with him. (Clearly my reluctance was my issue.)

Reluctantly, I sent him a brief email, to which he responded, *Maybe I can convince you to write more often?*

But even though Mark encouraged me to practice persistency by calling Keith daily, I only did this a few times. Each one-on-one exchange I had with him felt very awkward. Whenever I saw him in person, I felt like I was under a microscope. I often hesitated even to ask a question in a forum, as though it would reveal too much about my issues—as though Keith could see into my soul. I was flattered that he saw me on the same level as the senior executives, but the thought of one-on-one time with him made me anxious as he asked me to join him for walks or invited me to participate in different business opportunities, like an initiative to recruit sorority girls from local campuses. I secretly didn't think his other business ideas were any good, so I kept my distance. Besides, there was nothing I wanted to talk with him about. In forums, Nancy would tell us to ask Keith only things that were worthy of his time. If the question we presented was something we could learn from another coach or on Wikipedia, we weren't supposed to waste his time.

The one time I did go on a walk with him, I'd accepted the invitation because I was having trouble growing my coachees and keeping them on the Stripe Path. I hoped that face time with Keith would help me gain some wisdom. During that walk, we stopped at Nancy's house to watch videos on cell regeneration and how we can make limbs grow. It was so random, and I think he was just grappling for a topic to connect with me about. "Actually," I said, turning away from the video, "I was wondering if you could help me figure out how I can be growing more of my coachees to become leaders in the organization."

He peeled his attention away from Nancy's computer and turned to me. "Why would anyone want that when you make it look so hard?"

He was giving me feedback that I appeared to be "suffering" in my work, saying that my getting visibly stressed out was a deterrent that kept other potential coaches from wanting to grow. As usual, Keith was trying to intimidate me into submission and test my obedience. But I never trusted him enough to let him get close.

Despite my challenges, we were still thriving, and I hoped to be promoted from a yellow sash to orange, but the upper ranks told me I needed to keep working on my control and dependence issues. "Thank you for the feedback," I'd say . . . even though my reaction inside was, *What the fuck!* It seemed so unfair that while I excelled far beyond two of the promotion criteria—how many courses I'd completed and *how many people* we were enrolling in the Vancouver community!— their subjective assessment of how well I was mastering my emotional issues kept holding me back. What did Keith and Nancy want? For all of us to become perfect human beings? I respected the two of them so much professionally, but the feeling that they would never promote me was so intensely frustrating. I knew, however, that if I questioned it, it would impede my chance of progress even more.

To earn my living, I used the weekly Goals Lab to break into the voiceover community. I tried to set aside my concerns about advancing in the organization or how I could get paid steadily, focusing instead on how some members of the Vancouver community were impressed at the way I was building my career. When I took a deep breath with this perspective, I remembered I was becoming an integral part of something great. Through Sara Bronfman's connection to the Dalai Lama, Keith had recently traveled with Sara and Nancy to Dharamsala, His Holiness's residence in India, where they convinced him to speak at a NXIVM event.

I got to be up-close to this, as I was invited to attend the big event in downtown Albany. At the last minute, the Dalai Lama's trip was cancelled. Yet again, I returned to Vancouver in disappointment. I didn't find out why His Holiness had changed his mind, but I learned that after more talks, he'd finally agreed to come to Albany.

This time I couldn't fly out again to attend, but his appearance was all over the local news. This was an exciting time, with us Espians feeling legitimized by such a widely respected spiritual figure, as one of the photos from his visit showed His Holiness onstage, placing a white scarf over Keith's head. This was known to be a great spiritual honor. (Years later I would hear a rumor that the Bronfmans had allegedly contributed one million dollars to the Dalai Lama's foundation to seal the deal.) Keith was writing a book and the Dalai Lama had agreed to write the foreword—a major endorsement of Keith and NXIVM by His Holiness.

However, in the midst of all this excitement, a few articles had begun to appear in well-known news outlets like the *New York Post,* suggesting that some of Keith's senior leaders had confronted him about secret operations they believed were taking place. Barbara Bouchey, who'd been my sales mentor, suddenly left NXIVM along with a group of other executive-level coaches, many of them from the Tacoma center. In the headlines, this group of women were dubbed "the NXIVM Nine." From what I could gather from the wisps of quiet conversation I heard from Nancy and some of the other senior-level members, this group was accusing Keith of having sexual relationships with women on his executive board, and demanding money they claimed he owed them.

The story coming to us from the top was that Keith had tried his best to help Barbara, but she'd gone crazy and tried to extort money from him. We were told that for the sake of the organization, we had to cut contact with her as it simply would not be honorable to engage with her in any way as her tactics were destructive and violent to our community. Any further clues I got came from Mark, who was the only person I could talk to when I had a concern. "Why doesn't Keith just formally address the negative press?" I asked. Mark was receiving the same response from the senior-levels that I was, which was, "If you wrestle with a pig you both get dirty, but the pig likes it." It was a jab at mainstream media, personifying it as a filthy animal. Any coverage was quickly dismissed as being part of the smear campaign led by Barbara Bouchey. I believed what Lauren had told me about the NXIVM Nine: "Barbara was in love with Keith. Hell hath no fury like a woman scorned."

Looking back, I wish I had asked more questions. Instead, Nancy and Mark Vicente traveled out to the West Coast to do damage control.

As a group we gathered to watch *The Contender*—a film about a senator who's accused of sexual deviance in her past but refuses to answer or respond to the allegations. The film promoted upholding one's principles, as at the end the senator revealed she did not actually participate in the sex acts she was accused of. She chose never to respond to the accusations because she felt it was irrelevant to the political position she was vying for. I came away from the group screening feeling that all my questions had been answered. Focusing on someone's decisions in their personal life was irrelevant to the task at hand.

Shortly afterward, I learned that as a result of the accusations against Keith, the Tacoma center where most of those women had worked was being shut down. For me, this was bittersweet. The women in Tacoma had provided me with a place to develop my foundation in the organization. I'd also been close with Barbara Bouchey . . . but it wasn't a stretch for me to imagine that she had an unpredictable side. She'd been a significant figure in helping me get as far as I'd gotten, and a part of me wanted to reach out to her, but Nancy had been clear that we were required to cut off contact with Barbara immediately. I guessed that this was probably for legal reasons and, also, because we were expected to uphold NXIVM's principles. I cared about Barbara but also knew that if I wanted to stay in, I had to be careful not to associate with her. Not to have closure with someone I knew was totally against my gut instinct (and the way I was raised), but Nancy was the boss. Her orders left us with no question: Barbara was dead to NXIVM.

Now, the good news was that I could focus on growing the Pacific Northwest by building Vancouver, instead of still having to schlep down to Tacoma.

In retrospect, I can see the full chain of events. Finally, after all this time, they would promote me to proctor. It was part of their anticipation that all of this drama with the NXIVM Nine was coming down. The company needed me at the proctor rank in order to open a Vancouver center and keep the company operating in the region. Our growing enrollment numbers in Vancouver would more than make up for what they were losing in Tacoma.

This was a huge deal for me, for the Vancouver ESP community, and for NXIVM as a company. In July 2009, at the end of a forty-person intensive, the upper ranks promoted me in front of the entire coaching staff and our class. Mark was in town to help run that training, and for the promotion ceremony he Skyped in both Barb J. and Nancy. After the new students received their red stripe for completing the Five-Day, my two mentors paid me extensive tribute for all of my hard work as Mark placed that crisp orange sash around my neck. I had visualized this moment so many times!

Getting to proctor status meant I had reached official, paid coach rank. I had worked my butt off for four years to get there, taking thousands of hours of NXIVM coursework and recruiting hundreds of devotees. I'd *done* it. Reaching proctor gave me a sense of worth, esteem, and completion that I'd never in my life felt before. Via Skype, Nancy applauded me. Reaching that point made all the hardships I had gone through to get there, and any doubts I had, disappear. There was nothing holding me back.

Prior to this, we'd had no proctors in Vancouver or anywhere in Canada. My new status also meant I could open an actual center, as long as I did so in collaboration with a green sash. Because he also lived part-time on the West Coast and we'd been such close colleagues since I first enrolled, Mark was a natural partner. Around this time he was promoted to Green. Finally. It was go time.

We found a turnkey spot on Georgia Street in the middle of downtown Vancouver to serve as our permanent center. The space was a basement suite, with a rent of $6,000 a month, located next door to a spa. You'd enter on the street level and descend a flight of stairs, where it was extremely dark but there were good lamps, along with contemporary furniture that I bought myself after hiring an interior decorator from the community to consult. It was exactly what we needed. I will never forget the ribbon-cutting ceremony. Nancy even flew in, which was a rare treat. We threw a huge party, and a ton of Vancouver influencers came to celebrate. I was so proud to welcome our members into a space we could finally call our own. Even when we gathered on

Saturdays, the room was full. A couple of the younger members volunteered to help me set up and tear down. Everyone looked for some way to play a part. Now each time I traveled to Albany, Nancy would tell our colleagues that my recruitment work was exemplary. "If every city had a Sarah . . ." she'd say, and Lauren would give me an inconspicuous wink. I loved when they related to me at their level.

By fall 2009, our center was bustling. While Albany's center had a typical maximum of three students per class, in Vancouver we were bringing in eighty people a night. The center had a vibe of young entrepreneurs who were growing and sharing. Groups of like-minded individuals were working on their goals and pushing each other to be better. We were like a cool young church, buzzing with inspiration and activity.

I learned, however, that there was a limit to how "in" you really were. Around this time, Clare Bronfman had been named CFO because as I remember it, Keith said he appreciated that her lack of formal education made her a "flexible thinker." Once she invited me to a birthday party for Nicki Clyne that she was throwing at one of her homes in Albany. I told her that I'd be in town, but my friend Paige from the original *Artist's Way* group was traveling with me. "You don't mind if Paige comes with me to the party," I asked Clare. "Do you? She and Nicki are good friends from Vancouver."

"Actually . . ." I remember her saying in her King's English lite, that the party was to be held at her house, and she didn't really care to have Paige there.

OK, I got it. Paige and I opted not to attend. This was one of several instances that demonstrate why I never grew close with Clare. I felt the whole exchange was the opposite of what we were trying to build: humanity and community. It was a minor exchange, but I was so pissed that I asked one of the senior coaches to try to help me work it out with an EM—except through that process, we determined that I was the one being anti-humanitarian by trying to obligate Clare to host my friend. I ended up apologizing to Clare. "I'm so sorry I tried to obligate you," I said. That was the level of the mind-fuckery. Anytime I had an experience like this, I sometimes went to Mark, but was always careful to frame the issue in a way that was at-cause. "I'm having an issue," I'd tell him. "Can you help me with it?" Other than Mark, the only person I felt safe sharing this kind of thing with was Barb J. She never showed outright disloyalty to Clare or any other members, but sometimes by the careful way she phrased an answer or the tone in her voice while she listened, I knew she knew that sometimes there were some strong personalities at play.

Barb J. was the only one who respected my feelings and opinions. She never called me out for being straight-up wrong. And also, my own sense was that Clare hadn't been named CFO because of her open mind. I believed she'd been appointed to that role because she was bankrolling the company, and Keith wanted to keep her loyal to him. This was why, no matter what, I couldn't disagree with her. As I saw it, she was the money, and that gave her power over the rest of us.

I'd never really connected with Clare, but there were other members of the community I was growing closer to, like another actor whom I'd met shortly after I first joined the organization. Anthony Ames was a handsome American former college football quarterback, but he was so much more than an athlete. In some of the trainings we attended together, I'd noticed his confidence and intelligence. He'd gotten a degree in history from Brown University and was the kind of guy you would want on your team when you played one of those trivia games at a bar. He also had a really raw sense of humor, a mixture of Norm Macdonald and David Letterman, as he always found the line of appropriateness and then crossed it. One day we were chatting, and he totally charmed me. "I think we should go out," he said. I couldn't say no. The way things had been going with work, I was just loving life. I felt totally excited to see where it might go.

Everybody called him Nippy, from his middle name, Nippert, his mother's maiden name. He was also sweet and protective while emotionally evolved in a way that made it clear that he really respected the women in the company. I was enjoying our fun, lighthearted, long-distance relationship between Vancouver and New York City. We were two enthusiastic, driven people who shared a commitment to personal growth and human evolution inside NXIVM. Nippy had been a college football quarterback at an NCAA Division One school and had gone on to pursue acting. He was good-looking and charismatic, but also smart and tuned-in. We kept our relationship on the down low for a while, as we knew the upper ranks probably wouldn't approve. "Oh!" Barb J. said when after a few months I confided in her that we were seeing each other. "You are dating the quarterback?" Barb had taken over as my main coach when Barbara Bouchey left. I knew she was ribbing me, but I didn't care: Nippy was so creative, sweet, and ambitious, and we were having a good time.

So for me, this budding relationship and the opening of the Vancouver center were effective distractions from what had happened with the NXIVM Nine. Instead of entertaining any feeling of doubt, my focus was on how well things were working and how thrilling this all was. Mark Vicente and I started traveling to do Five-Days in Los Angeles at the homes of famous people in Los Feliz and Malibu. Our brand was slick, and A-list celebrities were taking our trainings. We didn't have enough local staff based down there, which meant I was able to fly Nippy in from New York to help coach. We were seeing each other often, we were rubbing elbows with extremely influential and recognizable people, I was earning good money—there were a few months when I was making upward of $20,000—and the whole thing was so glamorous and fast-paced and just plain *cool*.

Granted, I was putting most of my income back into the trainings to continue to drive enrollment, pay for flights, lend people money to take the trainings, and do whatever I had to do to keep growing the company on the West Coast, but I found that even my acting career was unstoppable in a way it had never been before. I'd recently landed some leading roles, including a film that made it into the Toronto International Film Festival. I felt like everything in my life was falling into place. At this point, I had also saved up enough to purchase my own cute one-bedroom condo in Vancouver. Just like all the women who lived in Albany, I'd reached the point of enough success to buy my own place. I was living proof: if you worked the tools in the way they were designed and stuck with the program, you would succeed. In a way I became a poster child for recruitment with the career, the money, the house, even the romance everyone wanted. If my sales techniques hadn't been convincing enough to attract new recruits, then my life definitely was.

SEGMENT I – Essence

My nature: all else is an effect of this

So far in life, I am the following: A human, a girl, a woman, a child, a student, a seeker, a parasite, a counsellor, a helper, an actor, an entrepreneur, a traveller and a creative artist.

To my family I am:
A daughter, sister, cousin, grandchild. A 1st Born x 2. I'm a squidbrain, a parasite, a source of joy, a creative partner and a friend.

To others in the world I am:
An inspiration, a leader, an OCD nutbar, a control freak, a good friend + listener. Superficial, fun, silly, smart, hot, geeky, unreliable.

My message and example to all people is: + positive. Sexy. Great Ass.
Be joyous, take responsibility, be the change. Follow your dreams.

SEGMENT VI – Mission Statement

The embodiment of my essence, purpose, and unencumbered values

Considering the above, my personal mission statement that reflects my essence, my purpose, and my values is:

My mission is to use and develop my creative and entrepreneurial skills to build value in a joyous, compassionate, inspiring way. To share the values of growth and introspection as I learn to know and love myself. And to create world changing film that inspires peace awareness, love and peace. and consequently evolve humanity.

Ethos brochure I received and exercises I completed

Keith Raniere playing volleyball, one of his favorite activities, 2005

With Nicki Clyne en route to Five-Day in Albany, 2005

Receiving my yellow coach sash from Dawn Morrison, 2005

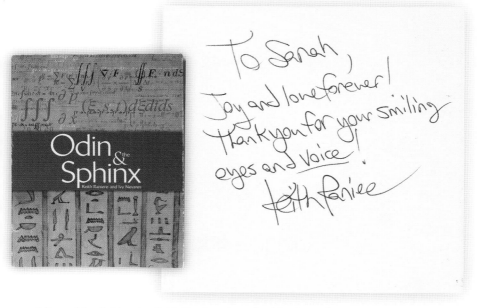

Odin and the Sphinx, by Keith Raniere, inscribed by the author

Opening an Ethos class in our Vancouver center with Mark Vicente

With Allison Mack in England, 2007

With Nancy Salzman and Barb J. in Vancouver, 2009

With Lauren Salzman at my wedding weekend brunch, 2013

Exchanging our wedding vows with Lauren as our officiant, 2013

Barb J. holding my son, 2014

With Pam Cafritz in Fiji, 2015

With the green team on a boat during V-Week, 2016

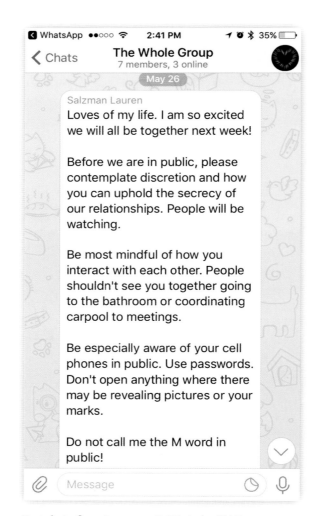

‹ Chats

The Whole Group
7 members, 3 online

May 26

Salzman Lauren

Loves of my life. I am so excited we will all be together next week!

Before we are in public, please contemplate discretion and how you can uphold the secrecy of our relationships. People will be watching.

Be most mindful of how you interact with each other. People shouldn't see you together going to the bathroom or coordinating carpool to meetings.

Be especially aware of your cell phones in public. Use passwords. Don't open anything where there may be revealing pictures or your marks.

Do not call me the M word in public!

Message

Text chain from Lauren to DOS circle, 2017

CHAPTER SEVEN

EFFORT STRATEGIES

2010
LOS ANGELES

With all of the company's traction and growth, the executive board decided that this was an opportune moment to raise the cost of our Ethos classes. I tried to fight this, to keep Ethos affordable for the community I had built. Clare's response was that I should stop enrolling struggling actors and focus on enrolling a different echelon—people who can invest more money in their personal growth.

I wanted to punch her through the phone. I was actually a higher rank than she was, but as soon as she became CFO, any matter regarding money, sales, or business had to go through her. When I had a student in Vancouver who was sick in the hospital and couldn't attend an intensive, Clare said maybe she'd look at whether she could give them their deposit back.

"No, Clare," I said. "Give them all their money back!"

Another challenge that arose a few years later, stemming from the company's desire to grow profit, was that Keith launched a whole new series of courses under the umbrella of Ultima, high-level, specialized studies focusing on specific areas of professional expertise. They included:

- *The Source,* for students who wanted to become professional actors.

- *The Knife Media,* to learn about media ethics and how to evaluate news sources in an ethical manner—based on data, not on opinion or projections.

- *Ethicist,* which was supposed to teach you to ethically evaluate and make ethics-based decisions.

- *exo/eso,* a combination of yoga, pilates, and other mat-based fitness disciplines.

- *Reverence,* a mash-up of all the emotionally focused modules from previous trainings. This was for anyone who wanted to feel more at-cause or wanted to get better at state control.

Keith was scouring the community for members with a high level of expertise to develop curricula. These courses were to be taught by professional actors and actresses, fitness teachers and dancers, journalists, even medical doctors. It was NXIVM's version of a MasterClass offering, with enrollees willing to pay thousands to participate.

The only problem was that these trainings hadn't actually been created yet. Students from the various Ethos branches, including Los Angeles and Mexico, volunteered to relocate to Albany in order to train with Keith directly and have the privilege of learning from his profound business acumen while developing these trainings with him.

I was invited to help create The Source, for people who wanted to learn skills in performing and presenting. I attended a few meetings in Albany and considered renting a place there but frankly wasn't eager to make a permanent move from Vancouver. I loved my city. I also wanted to be close to my family, and secretly, I feared that if I settled in Albany, the senior levels would want me to be involved in a way that would cause me to lose the autonomy I possessed in operating my own branch. The Source would eventually become Allison Mack's responsibility, and from the beginning I was relieved my name was never on it.

All of these courses were selling so well because the company had exploded since the NXIVM Nine had left. Breaking into Hollywood had opened a lot of doors for us, and the energy at our Vancouver center was busy and fun. Even though he would later deny it, the company used it as a selling point that Richard Branson had apparently taken one of the courses on his private Necker Island. I had spent so much of my life wanting to fit in and feel included, and now I'd proven myself. I believed they were being truthful—and if so, that meant I was among the elite not only in NXIVM, but in the world.

As the executives brought me into their fold, I'd noticed that Lauren and Nancy Salzman had a particular way of gossiping that made it sound like they were concerned only about the "issue" a subject was working in ESP—except that they were really spreading insider dirt. Nancy was privately coaching Hollywood stars who required strict confidentiality contracts, but she would disclose information to us about their divorces, their heartbreak, and their personal traumas. In a way, I didn't *want* to know. It felt surreal and a little troubling to be so close to the president of the company and to realize how willing she was to share private information about such public figures. If Nancy betrayed these clients' trust regarding extremely sensitive matters *and* when the legal stakes were high, then what on Earth was she willing to say about *me*? My trust in her started to waver.

But I had to admit, there was something about it that also felt very exclusive. Nancy would share details that tabloids and their readers would have paid a lot of money for. We were the only ones in the world, perhaps apart from their therapists, who knew what was actually going on inside the lives of some of these figures. That actress who broke up her co-star's marriage in real life? Yep. From what Nancy would convey, she was as crazy and insecure in real life as we guessed.

The gossip was lowbrow, but the information we gathered wasn't the only exclusive access that came with being part of the inner circle. Once, the Bronfman sisters came to Vancouver to pick me up in their jet en route to a training in Alaska. They had to stop in Vancouver to refuel and called me at the last minute and asked me to join them. This was very exciting—to be flown in a private jet to Alaska! I never could have imagined that this would be my life.

Now I'd become one of the star salespeople within NXIVM. With my thousands of hours of coursework I knew the material inside and out, and I could find the gem in every course that would draw people to enroll. Between my own direct enrollees and all the people they'd recruited, my team and I enrolled hundreds of people. I'd reached the highest closing rate in the whole company.

By now I'd grown obsessed with enrolling people. Every single thing I did had that undercurrent. When my interior decorator came to brainstorm ideas for my new home, I asked myself: *Would this person be interested in ESP?* But I didn't see it as doing a sales job on someone. I saw it as growing our community and changing the world while being in service to those new enrollees who wanted to make the most of their lives. I'd begun a habit of checking in with old friends to ask how they were doing, and whether there might be something more they were looking for. Some shied away from the program or said maybe they'd try it another time; others were curious about how I was doing so well and figured maybe it was worth a try. One friend's husband stood up and flat-out told me I was part of a cult, and I responded by saying that he was entitled to his opinion but clearly the program was working for me. Another friend turned down my initial invitation to come to a Five-Day, but a couple years later when she and her husband split up, she contacted me and said she'd been struggling in life and was interested in enrolling.

Anyone who took the Five-Day, which we were offering every other month now, almost always registered for the Eleven-Day. Because of all the ways the program had touched and transformed my life, I believed I was delivering a very authentic, meaningful service by inviting people to join us.

This was common in NXIVM. It became a way of living, the lens through which you viewed every relationship and decision. It took five years for my dad to take his first Five-Day, which drove a bigger wedge between my stepmom and me. But I wasn't going to let that be my problem. My dad had seen the changes in me and wanted that for himself. He saw how I had gained a stronger sense of confidence and an ability to handle conflict with ease. He was hoping to get rid of his negative self-talk and was committed to bettering himself. We agreed that if my stepmother had been at-cause, she'd be aware that her issue with ESP wasn't about me or my dad—it was her own issues and fears.

Truthfully, I had my own fears and challenges. I could barely keep up with the workload to keep the center running. I hired an assistant to help me stay on top of the administrative tasks. She was very sweet and hard-working, but my center was never her top priority. When she chose to do other things, I would repeat what Mark told me when I didn't attend something in Albany. "If that's your highest value," I'd say, "then go ahead and do it."

I was tough on my assistant—but I needed to see more hustle. If I'd been given an opportunity to get a salary when I started, I would have jumped through flaming hoops to do whatever the senior levels asked. In fact, I'd done that even when I wasn't getting paid.

I could feel that I had become more demanding since joining the company, because I had raised my standards. But, this was growth, right? My performance and my team's (and that of everyone at the center) had to be the absolute best because we had big goals in the world. I was responsible for so much within the organization and OK, *maybe* I was sometimes high-strung about the pace we ran at and what we had to deliver . . . but that's because I'd proven I could accomplish a lot. Bringing new people into this company and inspiring them to stick with their personal growth had become my purpose, and it put me on the radar of all these powerful people in the company. Even my acting career had become secondary. At this point, Nippy and I were dating casually, and, with that orange sash around my neck, I was focused on making my way to green. NXIVM was everything to me.

CHAPTER EIGHT

FLIP

2011

I looked at anyone who wasn't on board with my way of being either as just someone who was not into personal growth or, if they were critical about it, as a hater. I'd so internalized the principles of NXIVM that the psychological techniques they taught us to use in the program became my way of operating in interpersonal relationships. In retrospect, this could be used to both help and abuse, depending on your intent. The good way of using the tools was that we always had a quick and efficient way of problem-solving, looking for options, and moving through challenges. The negative aspect was that if and when anyone had a reaction and got upset, I could easily flip it around by suggesting that the person get an EM or talk to their coach.

In NXIVM, the tacit belief was that the lower-level individual was most likely the one causing the problem or having the issues. As I grew more adept at the organization's way of managing others' behavior (which I now see was a toxic way of relating), I saw this as my mastery of the program. The senior levels did it to me and I did it to others, and I later learned it was one of the features that defined it as a cult—the "closed-loop system of logic." In other words, no complaint from a lower-level individual was valid because the response was always, "What are you making it mean?" or "I think you are vested"— the NXIVM word meaning reactive or in need of circumstances being different—"and should probably get an EM before we talk further about that." In other words, if you speak up about anything you're not comfortable with, it's because of *your* issue. There was no way to give feedback to the upper ranks—Lauren, Nancy, or Keith especially—because they controlled your position in the organization.

What do you make it mean? This was one of the most overused and misused phrases within NXIVM. Senior leaders could use it to undermine our instincts, and our gut reactions. I can retrospectively see how NXIVM's framework and tools were designed to take all of that away. Senior leaders viewed any questioning of the content as defiance. This should have been more troubling, especially for someone like me, whose parents had put so much effort and intention into raising me to think for myself and to be kind to others. But this is where it got muddy: the helpful result of the curriculum was that it did teach us to think differently than how we were raised, to ask more questions rather than blindly accept convention, and to have more peace in our minds—as long as we didn't question the curriculum. By asking someone "What do you make it mean?" you suggest that the problem is *them* . . . not what they're reacting to. This was a constant reminder of the person's Inner Deficiency, the unique flaw that each of us was tasked with evolving. And that belief in an Inner Deficiency is what had hooked so many of us to stay in NXIVM and continue to work to fix something that was never broken to begin with.

Around this time, Keith and the senior-level leaders designed a system of consequences to hold members in the community more accountable. If it was determined that we had "failed" to uphold a commitment, we were required to fill out a "breach form," a one-page sheet that read like a Catholic confession, complete with self-criticism, requests for forgiveness, and the acknowledgment that one's most problematic "life issue pattern" had gotten in the way of advancement in the program and in life. Everyone hated doing breach forms because when you were really dedicated to ESP, you understood that when you missed the mark you weren't only letting yourself down; in failing to hold yourself to your highest standard, you had let down the community, and in some cases, the whole world. The feeling was isolating and shameful.

Next, there would be what the company referred to as "penances." This concept was similar to the way the term was used in the Catholic church: a penance was an activity or practice you'd take on if you failed at a next step or goal. For example, if I wanted to get into better physical shape but for any reason did not follow through with my commitment to go to the gym, my penance might be to take cold showers every day for a week or sleep on the floor instead of in my bed. Another type of penance was what we referred to as "collateral," or something you valued that you would put on the line when making a commitment; for example, someone who was trying to write a book but had failed to meet their daily page count might commit to give $1,000 to an individual (as Keith believed that charities perpetuated dependence). The idea behind penances and collateral was that they had to be significant so that you would be compelled to do what you had committed to. This wasn't a nickel in a Mason jar every time you said a curse word. You had to put something sizable on the line, so the penance was more painful than not completing your commitment. To me, both seemed to promote self-punishment.

With these new policies in place and given the increase in prices for some of the courses over the past year or two, plus the exchange rate going up 30 to 40 percent on the dollar, enrollment began to lose some steam. But that just meant I'd work harder. Some of us tried to follow Keith and Clare's advice to target prospective enrollees who were a little wealthier than our former market of upwardly mobile young adults, and for a short time, this was a successful tactic. We had Oscar-winning film directors and other people to bring us credibility still registering for the Five-Day. Unfortunately, it was a hamster wheel because the rent of our center went up as well as our administrative fees. I felt like I was always treading water. But I never stopped working, coaching, growing, and recruiting. I was getting paid for the sales, but from the time I woke up in the morning and drove to the center, I was on the phone doing EMs, coaching, and working with my coachees.

I had morphed from the innocent young woman who had wanted to use the world stage for the greater good into what I now recognize as a puppet for the company. As a fledgling creative professional, of course I'd craved financial stability early in my career . . . but never before had I had this much security. Both the money and my work gave me their own kind of high. I had worked hard, and I wanted to enjoy the fruits of my labor with my friends. I felt like I was killing it. Lauren and Allison loved to buy designer brands like Marc Jacobs, and now I could actually shop with them. A luxury vehicle, expensive facial cleaners and creams, twelve dollars for a green juice when I went to visit Nippy in New York. Never before had I been able to buy almost anything I wanted. I was helping people and getting paid for it.

Nancy Salzman worked that same angle when she told me about Jness (pronounced *juh-NESS*) that was a newly revised version of the weekend workshop that many of us had taken back in 2006. Nancy told me the purpose of this cutting-edge curriculum would be to strengthen women's influence in the world, bond us women closer to each other, and address contemporary dynamics in male-female relationships.

Strengthening our influence was what Keith and Nancy wanted us to think this was all about. It was also in our twelve-point mission statement: "People control the money, wealth, and resources of the world. It is essential for the survival of humankind for these things to be controlled by successful, ethical people. I pledge to control as much money as possible within my success plan. I will always support the ethical control of these things."

I'd come to live by that mission statement so faithfully that I didn't know how to relate to people anymore. By constantly being in coach and sales mode, I'd reached the level of three-stripe orange. From the first time I'd ever recited the mission statement at the Five-Day, I'd been taught to believe that it would be better for the world to keep money in the hands of ethical people. Later I would realize how naive I was to think that the company was ever ethical at all.

A lot of people got to coach, and a handful of people made it to proctor and stagnated there . . . but with one more stripe I'd be promoted. I could taste my green sash, but still needed one more stripe to reach it. This was reminiscent of the way I'd been stuck on my yellow sash, so I was used to this nonsense by now. I'd actually enrolled enough people to get a blue sash, but the upper ranks determined that my emotional issues kept getting in the way.

No matter what level you reached, Keith, Nancy, and Lauren, in consultation with some of the most senior coaches, kept moving the goal posts to make it harder for you to reach the next level. I've since learned that Scientology has a similar business model where in any phase of training, a student (like me) had to go back and buy all the textbooks that they'd already read because each new annual edition made very slight modifications to the structure and the teachings.

I had a massive freakout when I found out that Lauren and the education board were changing the criteria for learning how to conduct EMs. We learned that we would all have to start at the beginning and move through the EM methodology that I had already paid thousands of dollars to learn over hundreds of hours of training. "But I've already gotten here, to level five," I said. "Do I really have to recertify?"

"If you're really that good," said my evaluator in the EM path, "it should be easy to reach this point again." Annoyed but committed, I went through all the coursework again. "I know," Barb J. empathized. "Hang in there. You know I'm here to help you." But even with the support of the senior coaches, I never reached level five in the EM training a second time. Somewhere inside me, I knew trying was pointless. I also secretly felt I was helping people just fine without the certification.

The worst part was that for us to question it meant we were being suppressive or entitled, or mad-dogging our coach. Accepting what-is is one of the pledges we made in the NXIVM mission statement: *There are no ultimate victims. Therefore, I will not choose to be a victim.* Now I can see how messed up this is and try to warn others—never join an organization with subjective standards for promotion.

I'd proven myself as dedicated and successful to all the senior-level members, but I still hadn't received a promotion from an orange sash to a green. Once again, the senior-level leaders explained that my control and other patterns were holding me back. At this point, I had EM'd the shit out of most of those. Why had Lauren and Mark gotten promotions to green, and I hadn't?

Remember that early on, they'd told me that people could get to the next level in six months, but I learned that only one person in NXIVM history had done that. It would take six years for me to learn that the reason I wasn't promoted was something they wouldn't say: they knew that I was too vocal ever to be one of their cheerleader-puppets. Control issues? NXIVM had sold us on the idea that we had authorship in our lives, and then disrupted our reasoning process to take our personal control away. They'd seen that every time I'd felt genuinely uncomfortable, I would tend to say something. What they dubbed my Inner Deficiency, my "life issue," may have been their fear that one day I'd get close enough to figure them out and blow the whistle.

CHAPTER NINE

OBEDIENCE

2013

In 2013, NXIVM kicked off the first Jness "tracks" for both men and women. Up until now, Jness had been offered exclusively to women in weekend workshops that cost only $550. These new tracks, in contrast, would cost $15,000 for three eight-day trainings. Keith would be teaching the first iteration in this new track, so all of the upper ranks and dedicated Espians jumped to take it.

For a while, the men in ESP had been asking for their own curriculum like the women's. Seeing a business opportunity, Keith immediately began to develop an accompanying program focused on the male experience. The new male-targeted course would be called "Society of Protectors" or SOP—and even though it sounded more like an R-rated video game than a class, I, like a lot of Espians, was intrigued about the content. Keith quickly developed an SOP course that women could take alongside the men called "SOP Complete." SOP Complete was like a boot camp so that women could experience what it's like to be raised as a boy in our society—expected to be strong, forbidden to cry, considered weak if they showed emotion. We were told it would help us to understand the men in our lives. Keith would be teaching these original co-ed courses himself, which didn't happen often.

After we took the trainings from Keith, Nippy became a prom-inent leader of the men's program. He'd been chosen to act on the SOP governing board—in part because he was one of the few men who was able to consistently run the weekends, eventually bringing over 150 men into the SOP fold. He was also a natural fit, having been captain of his athletic teams in high school and a college quarterback, and being obsessed with reading biographies about great leaders and presidents. Nippy was the perfect spokesperson. *If you look out into the world,* my boyfriend taught the men in the SOP lessons, *wouldn't you agree that our leadership is lacking a certain moral fiber that is necessary to move our society forward?*

Yes, because that's the base assumption that everyone who'd reached this level of ESP had bought into believing. It was the reason that Keith and Nancy had founded NXIVM in the begin-ning: because most people on the planet weren't living consciously in their relationships and other significant life choices. Like me, Nippy had years of experience in front of the room and was effective because he believed in what we were doing. His emotional connec-tion to the material made him very persuasive. That was how the company grew: Keith had well-intentioned people unwittingly push-ing his agenda. Nippy could sway a group of men with his sincere belief that the world needed this message. What I've come to realize is that just like the curriculum in ESP, there's what we *thought* it was teaching and what it was *actually* teaching. We were told that what we needed was a safe place to come together and look at our current indoctrination from society in order to evolve it. My per-sonal hypothesis in retrospect is that in looking at men and women and our roles, Keith was actually slipping in his own indoctrina-tion about what he wanted us to feel and believe about the opposite sex—grooming certain students of Jness and SOP to become his unwitting accomplices.

He used genetics to explain the distinction between men and women, claiming it was essential to right the imbalance of a male-dominant/female-influenced culture. The concepts of the SOP and Jness curriculum were supposed to do that. But in reality, SOP was a traditional way of viewing relationships, where men were the hunter-gatherers who protected women and women were the domestic damsels in distress who needed them. The curricula for Jness and SOP taught that in our society, men and women had separate roles and capabilities. Men were meant to be our heroes and protectors, and they had the wiring to spread their seed, which justified that sexual appetite. This set the foundation for Keith to rationalize his behaviors: men were wired for non-monogamy, while women were genetically dispositioned to stay with one man. Ultimately, Keith wanted to teach us that a woman's role is to obey a man. He liked to tell a joke about a young couple who got married in the olden days and left the church in a horse-drawn cart. When the horse tripped, the man shot his gun in the air and counted: "One!"

The next time the horse tripped, he'd shoot into the air again. "Two!"

His newlywed bride asked him, "What are you doing?"

"I'm keeping the horse in line so he knows who's in charge."

The bride pouted. "That's so cruel."

At that, the man shot his gun in the air while looking at her and shouted: "One!"

When we heard this joke, some of the women in the group turned to each other and grimaced. Others, like Clare Bronfman, would take careful note and later request a session to "debrief" with us women after class to suggest ways we could improve and be more obedient to men. Once, I remember her gathering us in the Apropos parking lot, recommending that we all learn to dress more appropriately, like she did: in slacks and simple shirts that wouldn't show any tempting cleavage. I couldn't help but giggle when one of my students from Vancouver whispered, "Who made *her* our leader?" It was true. Clare demanded a respect that she hadn't earned.

Both programs overlapped in overall content and in the way they were scheduled so that anyone who was interested could take both of them. And many did, because the opportunity to learn the content directly from Keith was so unusual and exciting. After I left, I'd hear recordings as he was developing his ideas for the teachings that exhibited how extremely fucked-up his thoughts really were. He'd used graphic, vulgar language, sometimes tacitly promoting violent sex. One video showed him using words and phrases like "getting fucked" and that men are "hungry fucking beasts" over and over. In a training before one group, Keith was actually captured on tape stating that women enjoy being "fucked" in a man's worst state of anger.

Meanwhile, the promise that Jness would evolve us to set the archetype for the modern woman was what made me, and so many other young women, buy into the concept—that, along with the insights about guys that we were gaining from SOP Complete. For the men as well as the women, Keith and Nancy were selling a promise— except that the promise to the women and the promise to the men conflicted. Jness training was supposed to make us women stronger and help us develop character, and while SOP was allegedly creating a men's movement, it actually proved to be a platform for Keith's latent mysogyny. At the time, no one knew Keith's true purpose of this belief system.

If we hadn't been conditioned to dismiss our personal judgment, following the way NXIVM urged us to "suspend judgment in order to explore concepts," I probably would have walked out of some of these lessons. The upper ranks often reminded us: if you were uncomfortable, it meant you were "doing it right." With this in mind, I stayed put, though I struggled with it.

Besides, if I didn't agree with something: who could I go to? When a boss makes an off-color joke or a remark that could be insensitive or offensive, what do you do—especially when it's the company's founder and leader? It's not like NXIVM had an HR department. Anyone who spoke up would never get promoted. A few students who attended those early Jness trainings left on day one or two, never to take NXIVM curriculum again. But for those of us who were willing to sit through Keith's talks, our hope was that this would make us leaders in the company, and leaders in the world.

It's easy for me to see now that under the guise of offering courses to help the sexes understand each other, Jness and Society of Protectors were actually employing stereotypes and extreme generalizations. Keith taught that we women were complainers, that we were "princessy," that we were wishy-washy and didn't follow through or show up to things for meaningless reasons like having menstrual cramps. "How would you feel if a man canceled a meeting because of cramps?" Nancy read from a Jness briefing. "Not a real man, right? Only we women do that kind of thing." On top of that, these two programs sloppily conflated being male with the notion of masculinity, and being female with femininity, while ignoring any sexual orientation or gender identification that wasn't associated with straight men or women.

The whole thing was so narrow-minded. I recall Keith saying that some women are so clueless that they walk too slowly on the sidewalk. *Wow*, I thought. *I've noticed that!* It was extremely overgeneralized, but I'd observed that in some cases it was true. I think many of us women were captivated because we could see ourselves in some of the examples he mentioned. That saying, "The greatest lies have a grain of truth"? That's exactly what this was. As he called attention to the weaknesses in some women, I became conscious that I didn't like some of these aspects of myself and the women I knew. *Keith's right*, I thought. *Some women are just oblivious.*

Meanwhile, Nippy and I both watched how some women cruelly forced these ideas on each other. I noticed that what we were learning was making us feel worse about ourselves, not stronger, and we were starting to adopt these misogynistic ideas. As I bought into Keith's teachings about men, women, and our interpersonal relationships, I could feel my love for my sisterhood eroding. On some level I knew that Jness and SOP weren't encouraging a loving understanding between the two sexes. They were driving us apart. I heard people making disparaging comments about the opposite gender—if a man was struggling to connect emotionally someone might say: "Typical man! He can't feel." A man might publicly point out how a woman wasn't committed or following through on a project because she lacked strength and character.

After about a year into the Jness trainings, I started to excuse myself and step out to check emails or do other work. "You're missing the chance to really go deep and feel these concepts," Pam Cafritz told me. At times like this, Barb J. didn't push. For me there came a point when the material just wasn't resonating with me. I'd listen for one session and then go work on something else. I knew that if I kept closing enrollment sales, they wouldn't press me to engage more than I was inspired to.

Inside our relationship, Nippy and I joked at how the courses we were taking played out between us, about my willingness to be "obedient" to him. We made light of what we were learning, not realizing how the community in Albany was taking things to the next level. We joked about the generalizations that were made in the curriculum about men and women, like memes on Instagram. But we were not aware how the women close to Keith were making this a way of life.

And we certainly didn't think that with these teachings we were priming our students to assume that women are supposed to please men. Neither of us believed that. We had no idea we were setting the stage for what would normalize a group of women to be coerced and groomed to have sex by force under Keith, or that we were preparing them to become his concubines. Starting with the NXIVM Nine, I'd heard murmurs about Keith sleeping with some of the members of NXIVM. I always stuck with the ESP basics and avoided invitations to join Keith in new ventures. But the truth is, as a student of Jness, I was part of the whole fucked-up system.

Keith had taught us all to worship him and now, even though I was unaware of it, he was preparing to use these teachings to his advantage and commit some of the darkest acts I'd ever heard of. They would happen to some of the people I had trained and some I cared about the most.

Including me.

PART THREE

BLOWING IT UP

2013–2017

CHAPTER TEN

SHARED VALUES

To me, you are my love in human form

You are all poetry, beauty, awe and joy.

In my every experience, there you are.

Behold my senses and self.

In practical life, I will always hold out my best for you against any and all adversity.

I will fill each moment with this promise remembering some-day one of these moments will be our last.

Keith had written the vows that Nippy and I used when we married in September 2013. We borrowed them from Mark, who had
recently married Bonnie, a fellow Espian who was a beautiful actress
and singer/songwriter. When we'd heard their vows months earlier,
we thought the words were perfect.

We wed in a private civil union in the spring of 2013, but the following September we wanted to host a proper affair with a ceremony
and a huge party for our families and our friends from NXIVM inside
the Shangri-La Hotel in downtown Vancouver.

That morning, the entrance to the hotel was flanked by tall floral
arrangements; the marble floors and chandeliers in the lobby glistened

while the main sitting area was adorned with large tropical bird of paradise plants.

I wanted everybody who attended to be dazzled—not only because it was our wedding day, but also because this would be the first time I would be meeting my new husband's parents. They lived between New York City and Atlanta and had five adult children, so with his travel and mine largely on the West Coast to host ESP workshops or to attend quick meetings in Albany, we hadn't yet locked down an ideal time to connect with his entire family. I was so nervous for all the planning to roll out just right . . .

. . . And I was intimidated. The moment I met the sophisticated Southern woman who'd just become my mother-in-law, I could tell that her all-American, upstanding son was the apple of her eye. Her children had always been her priority. I approached to hug her warmly—and while she was polite, I thought I sensed some disdain. It was as though she was watching her son in a situation she knew she couldn't control. Nippy had warned me not to worry about her judgment and had a great way of using humor to ease the tension. Still, I wanted to please her.

I couldn't tell if that perceived judgment had more to do with me, or with our group of friends—and the Espians had come out in full force to celebrate our marriage. More than sixty friends from all the NXIVM centers across North America had RSVP'd. Half of my bridesmaids were students in ESP, with Lauren Salzman serving as my maid of honor and our officiant. She and the rest of our bridal party were elegant in black satin, and I wore a knee-length strapless white cocktail dress. I'd just found out that I was six weeks pregnant, and Nippy and I were thrilled. Yet, the inability to drink alcohol was never an issue at a NXIVM event. Despite a mostly dry reception in one of the hotel's ballrooms, we owned the dance floor and even performed a flash-mob routine that a choreography company of fellow Espians from Mexico had taught us less than a month earlier at the annual V-Week.

Even though both my parents had dipped their toes in the water with ESP at different points, our wedding was a bit of a reckoning for my family, too. My extended family had no idea of the degree or depth of my involvement with NXIVM, and I could feel that both my parents and my in-laws didn't quite know what to make of us. My mom took quiet moments to express her sentiments softly to me, and everyone on both sides posed cooperatively for photos. But there was something I had silently asked them all to overlook: to pan around the room was to see plastic smiles pasted onto perfect faces with everyone from ESP looking so damn robotic that when I felt the eyes of my husband's parents on me, even I felt uneasy. I could tell it was unnerving for them, as well as my own parents, to see how happy we all acted—like, *What the fuck Kool-Aid are you guys drinking?* Nancy had flown in, but Keith had stayed in Albany because he didn't like to travel, unless it was for an occasional visit with the Dalai Lama. His absence might have made another couple feel blown off, but I was relieved. The only thing that would have made the whole thing feel even stranger would have been to have him there basking in the spotlight surrounded by his gaggle of devotees.

The following morning we hosted a brunch, where our photographer floated around, still snapping photos. He, like almost all of the vendors I'd hired, was a member of ESP. This was part of our philosophy: whether you needed a hairstylist, a mechanic, a financial planner, a florist, an undertaker—what*ever*—you agreed to shop inside the community and hire anyone who was a professional offering the services you required. NXIVM called it the Ethical Business Coalition, and I thought of it as our own little friendly economy. If we fed each other's bank accounts, then we gave each other the money necessary to stay in and keep taking ESP courses. I've always loved shopping local. In this context, I wanted people in my community to be making money, and I wanted to support them.

But as it was, our photographer was on it. I'd made up my breakfast plate at our buffet line and had slid into a seat next to Lauren, who was fresh-faced and curly-haired after letting her hair dry naturally that morning. When the photographer came around, I moved in close to Lauren and wrapped my arm around her. She grasped my fingers with her hand, but lightly, almost unenthusiastically . . . and gave a closed-mouth smile that was different from her usual full-face beam. As I review it now, I was so elated that even in the black-and-white image I can see the lines that form right at the point where my cheeks meet my eyes. My best friend had flown in to celebrate the happiest event in my life . . . but she doesn't look very happy.

Around this period in our friendship, the two of us had engaged in a conversation that struck at the heart of an issue that I knew Lauren had been debating for some time. Lauren wanted to have a baby. When I asked her why she wasn't making a move on that dream, she said it was "for the sake of the organization." I'd given her a look: *Huh?* We were both in our late thirties. Why was she letting the organization or anyone make that choice for her?

She'd always maintained this low profile about her love life—in fact, her romantic life itself was something that I as her friend worried about because it was all but nonexistent. I often recalled the time she'd revealed to me that she'd had a fling with somebody in NXIVM, but she traveled around so much that it could have been any guy at any one of the Ethos centers in Albany, Los Angeles, or Mexico. (I knew it wasn't likely to be Vancouver because I was too close with our members for any of them to have had a relationship with my best friend without my knowing.) When I pressed her about this decision, she shared with me that she and Keith had engaged in a long talk where he'd helped her see that the community was like her children. She'd determined that really was her highest value. When I heard this, I thought something was off. I thought she was making a poor decision but didn't mention it because she seemed settled in her thinking.

Meanwhile, Nippy and I were growing stronger. Neither he nor I knew what was around the corner or how important our loyalty to each other would become . . . but as the truth started to emerge, we now had this private space inside our life together to examine what would begin to expose itself. *In my every experience, there you are.* These were the words we'd conveyed to each other in the vows Keith had written, and it was so on point. Nippy and I were now witnesses to each other and all that we each would encounter. Though I am still figuring out even today what made sense from ESP and what didn't, these words were real.

After our wedding, we sold my apartment and bought a two-bedroom in Vancouver's Olympic Village, a neighborhood that had been renewed along the banks of the seawall that had been the site of the 2010 Olympics. Nippy wanted to return to the East Coast at some point, but for now we agreed that things at our Ethos center were steady and he'd support me in running it while he grew SOP Vancouver. We began to settle into our forever together . . . but while the company and community had all run so well for so long, things began to go terribly sideways—and there was no room for anyone to deny it.

It all started right around our wedding with the fact that Barb J. hadn't attended. Barb was my main point person in ESP since Barbara Bouchey had left. Over the past three years, she'd put aside her playfulness, however sharp, about my dating Nippy when she realized how serious we were. She didn't skip the wedding because she was opposed to our marriage—she'd become seriously ill.

It was so mysterious: within the upper ranks, a message was coming down—we were told from Keith and Nancy—that Barb had gone crazy (was it some kind of dementia? I wondered) and had gotten sick with brain cancer. No one from the upper ranks would go into detail about it.

Barb was incredibly important to me, and I'd push to do everything I could to help even though now, just weeks from delivering our son, I wasn't able to fly. I made a few phone calls and put her in touch with a holistic healer I knew through a friend, who instantly made arrangements to travel to Albany. He spent some time in Barb's home, putting her on a specific protocol with juices, dietary supplements, and healing herbs. I spoke with Barb while he was still with her, and she sounded more energetic and full of grit—more herself—than she'd sounded to me in weeks. The healer took the phone and said she was out of bed, functioning and walking around. She was even talking about going outside to take her two dogs for a walk. Walking and her dogs: I knew those were the things that made her the happiest. If she could focus on that, she could get through this. Right now, she was sounding so good.

But after a few days, when I called her, her voice sounded drained again, exhausted and losing hope. "What's wrong?" I asked. She told me that Keith had sent the healer away and put Barb on his own regimen. "Why?" I asked. "What are you taking?" I sat down on my sofa, knowing the pace of my heart wouldn't be good for my blood pressure this far into my pregnancy. I could tell she was too weak to say much more . . . and, as I understand now, too dedicated to say anything disparaging about Keith.

Shortly after I gave birth to our son, Barb J.'s health went swiftly downhill. That August we flew to Albany for V-Week, taking the three-month-old to visit her before heading up to the Silver Bay resort for my eighth year in a row.

In her home I took a picture of Barb J., one of my most beloved mentors of the past decade and of my whole life, as she held my infant in her arms. In the photo, her famous long hair had been totally chopped off and shorn close to her head. She'd always looked so tanned and sculpted, like a woman who grew all her vegetables and chopped her own wood . . . but here, she's pale and in some places bruised—purple marks on her wrists, her hands.

I climbed above her and hovered over the two of them to take the photo. I was intent on immortalizing this moment of love that Barb expressed to my son. In the image, he sucks a pacifier and looks at the camera while his head rests on his hand with his elbow bent, the same relaxed pose Nippy takes to in bed after a long day. Barb gazes down on him with her fingers on his heart, as if reflecting on the profundity of what it is to have your whole life ahead of you.

I cried when we left her that day, thinking how unfair it was that death should take someone who'd brought so much positivity to so many people's lives. Nippy drove us from there to Silver Bay, where I thought I might receive the fourth stripe on my orange sash—the final promotion before advancing to green.

What I didn't know was that the upper ranks were conspiring to transition the company at this time, and to motivate the community with more promotions than I'd ever seen. Instead of granting me the final stripe I needed before advancing to green, they had decided to send me straight there. The promotion ceremony would take place that week in front of the hundreds of people who were coming for V-Week. Inside the auditorium at Silver Bay on Lake George, Pam Cafritz strung the sash around me while the crowd, my husband, and my colleagues applauded. This was a big win. In that moment, I was motivated again. For the first time, I was part of the green team with my closest friends, including Mark and Lauren. It had taken me five years to move from orange sash to green. I was beaming.

There was just one thing missing: Barb J. She was dying at her home, not far from where we were. I stood there before the V-Week audience, thinking how for years Barb had coached me to this point. But when I'd seen her hours earlier, she'd looked to me like she'd been through a war.

Even though she never said so, I realize now that she had been.

CHAPTER ELEVEN

RAINBOW CHILD

In September 2014, just three weeks after she'd met our son and I jumped the ranks to green, Barb J. passed away. "Barb was really happy you finally got promoted," Lauren told me.

I was distraught, unclear about why Keith would have sent away the holistic healer I'd called in when Barb had begun to do so well on his protocol. What made it even more heartbreaking and perplexing for me was that the more senior executives seemed to hurry along a simple ceremony—and, worse, at moments chose not to remember her goodness but instead to call insensitive attention to what they identified as her faults. I flew back to Albany to attend the short memorial service they held at Apropos, where Lauren muttered under her breath, "Barb J. never worked her anger." She said it abruptly, dismissively, as if we were sitting in the pedicure chairs talking about someone we disliked instead of at the memorial service of a woman who had been a loving mentor to us both.

Barb J. had given her life to the community—*for* the community— and now her life was over. She'd been like a loving aunt to us both, and Lauren was disrespectful and hurtful. Weren't we supposed to be like family? And weren't we supposed to uphold each other and not overlay their issues onto their personhood? I didn't say anything in response. Lauren had been analytically critical of so many people we knew, as though because she was Nancy's daughter she understood people better than they understood themselves. It was as though the rules that applied to the rest of the community did not apply to Lauren.

Weeks went by. Nancy had paired me with a new coach. Alex Betancourt was a businessman and one of the owners of the Mexico City center. He was one their biggest influencers, close with some of the most notable movers and shakers there—including Emiliano Salinas, whose dad had once been the president of Mexico. However, I felt like Alex kept flaking out on appointments with me. When I'd try to pin him down to reschedule, he always gave some lame excuse for why he wasn't available. His lack of reliability allowed me to fly under the radar of the higher ranks, but without that consistent check-in I was feeling anxious. When I brought this to Nancy's attention, she promised to step in and coach me in Barb's place. As good as she was at teaching modules and working people through their issues, Nancy was infamous for overpromising and under-delivering.

With no one helping me "work my shit," I decided to focus on the Vancouver center and spend a lot of time thinking. Nippy and I went for long walks on the seawall, where we discussed losing Barb. I quieted my mind in yoga class. I spent some time in silence . . . and in doing so unearthed a memory about Barb J. that brought up some questions I had never allowed myself to consider before.

Six years earlier, in 2008, Barb J. had shown up in possession of something I'd never expected her to have: a baby. She'd explained this with a story about how a close friend in Michigan had gotten sick and died. She told us she was the godmother and had been called on to assume legal guardianship of the child. I talked to Barb often, and this seemed to have appeared from out of nowhere. Never before had I heard anything about this from her, but because I lived on the opposite side of the continent from Albany, it wasn't unusual for me not to have the full picture of what was going on in everyone's life. I sometimes heard bits of pieces of accounts like this from Lauren and Mark.

But now various publications were getting hold of the story. Again, we were reminded never to believe the media. The baby, a little boy, was named Gaelen. He became the first child exposed to the ESP training for children, called Rainbow Cultural Garden, which Keith developed just for him. Keith had arranged for Gaelen to have care-takers who were students in ESP from different countries. Their job was to speak to him in English, Spanish, Hindi, Russian, and more. I once heard Nancy brag that he was learning eleven languages and could speak in full sentences in all of them. When I was in Albany I would sit and take this child in—a precious, innocent little boy with elfen looks and questions in his eyes. I felt sorry for this little boy who had lost his mother, but for the months I was aware of the situation, I hoped that the intense caretaking he seemed to be receiving would be healing for him. I respected Barb J. for stepping in to make the best of a sad situation. I mean, how many little kids have a whole team of nannies?

I knew Gaelen as a baby, but when he suddenly disappeared a cou-ple of years later, there was a lot that didn't quite add up. The story the higher-ups gave us was that Kristin Keeffe, one of Keith's right-hand women handling legal issues for NXIVM, had taken over as Gaelen's primary care giver. They said she'd recently gone crazy and kidnapped Gaelen, and that the two of them were living on the streets.

Living on the streets? Where?!

Lauren said she had no idea. She seemed blasé about it. There was a collective shrug; no clear plan for any of them to make a single move to help this child. This was so disturbing. Why didn't they stop Kristin? A woman can't just kidnap a child. Had they reported this? Was anybody looking into it?

Kristin was crazy, they'd said—just the same as when Barbara Bouchey had left.

Now, when you Google it, you can find the articles from the *New York Post* with headlines like "Albany Cult Takes Orphan." But we'd been coached time and again not to believe the lies the press published about Keith. Mark asked me not even to read about him, and warned me that I wouldn't want to change my "thought object"—my internal representation—of Keith. Still: who was Gaelen? Where had he come from, and what had happened to him? He never returned.

One of the most powerful experiences when you become a mother is the feeling that you're now bearing the responsibility—and the urge—to fight for the well-being of every child on the planet. Late nights after Nippy had gone to bed, I would tiptoe into the living room and nurse. While my child and I relaxed, locking into each other's deep brown eyes, or as his lashes fluttered and his cheeks rounded back from my breast as he drifted off to sleep, I marveled at how our bond would be fundamental to the stability and security he'll feel about everything else in his life. "You're an incredible mother," my own mom told me when she saw how joyfully and naturally I'd taken to motherhood. I'd had to work so hard at every other role in my life. But this? Every time I soothed him to sleep or swaddled him in a towel to keep him warm right out of the bath, I felt like I was born to be a mom.

Our son was so wanted, so cared for, so cherished and safe. While sinking into the bliss of these moments, I would suddenly feel anger rising up: *Why hadn't anyone fought for Gaelen?*

Why hadn't I pushed harder for answers? We weren't supposed to talk about Kristin Keeffe, so I'd never felt free to ask the upper ranks what they made of the whole thing.

When I contemplated who I could ever really trust to help my son make his life decisions if anything ever happened to Nippy and me, I thought of Lauren. She was smart. She was so good with the tech and could help anyone like a ninja with a few sentences. She knew literally everything about my life, and we shared total trust. I had so much respect for her. Eventually Nippy and I decided to ask Lauren to be our son's godmother. It meant the world to me to see how she loved my little boy. She brought him generous gifts and would take selfies with him. She fawned over our son like he was her own child. Over the past ten years, we really had become what they'd always said: like family.

And family was what mattered most to me at this time. As Nippy and I embraced our life with our son, I could feel my priorities shifting. Attaining green was meaningful to me but it certainly did not compare with becoming a mother. This new era in our life, combined with losing Barb J., had begun to make me very subtly aware that I wanted to start distancing myself from the community.

But it was as though the upper ranks could sense that motherhood was threatening to pull me away. I started to feel more pressure from Albany for us to move there because they still wanted me to help lead the development of the Ultima curricula. I didn't want to be anywhere near it. By this point I had seen enough people move to Albany and drop off the face of the earth. All of the actors, like Nicki and Allison, who had moved there to "deepen their craft" had stopped auditioning altogether. I had also witnessed people giving up their lives for vague work exchanges that seemed like bottomless pits. Truthfully, I felt lucky that I'd dodged the company's pursuit by getting pregnant. I'd known very firmly that I wanted to have my child in Canada, as Nippy and I agreed that it was a more affordable place to give birth than the U.S. But somehow, I had anticipated that the senior levels would campaign to move us to Albany.

The upper ranks turned the Ultima invitation into a tremendous push for us to join them permanently. The executive team passed a message to me through Lauren that it was time for me to overcome my latest issue, which they'd decided was my "attachment to materialism and comfort." My pregnancy had felt like a valid reason to stay in Vancouver and avoid the shitshow that was Ultima. Not only was I supposed to be attending it, but as a field trainer I was also supposed to be filling the training with students. But no one could tell me the cost, how long it would last, or what it would entail. Keith was teaching it, Clare spouted sanctimoniously, asking me why that wasn't enough for me to enroll more of my students.

I wasn't going to move a muscle. Things at our center were still going well. While I respected Keith's work as our leader, I thought the format they were creating for Ultima was totally ridiculous, and the prices they finally decided on, up to $10,000 for a training, were a rip-off. My bullshit meter had gone off when I saw that Keith had promised some of the professionals he'd brought to Albany that building the Ultima curriculum would take no more than two months—but some ended up staying two years! Some had gone to Albany and then never left.

The Ultima project seemed to be a black hole for young talent, and to be honest, I had doubts about whether these professionals were even getting paid for the time and skill they were putting into it. One young guy had been a successful journalist who actually quit his job working for Bloomberg to develop curriculum for The Knife, the ethical media course. Nippy and I told a close friend not to go to Albany, but she didn't listen, accepting a promise from Keith to work with her on her hockey career. Since when does Keith know anything about hockey? we wondered. "Get it in writing," I told her. "What's the exchange? Do you have a contract?" She wound up in deep debt, never addressing her hockey career but instead working without pay for two years to help build one of Keith's new companies that never got off the ground.

When Keith had asked me to contribute to the Ultima acting class, I'd declined, feeling that you couldn't package years' worth of theatrical training and acting experience into a workshop that people might attend for a few weeks. I also intuitively didn't trust that Keith knew anything about acting. Allison Mack, who by now had left her television career in Los Angeles to buy a house in Albany and starred in a few videos to promote programs like Jness, had stepped up to lead the development of The Source, targeted at wannabe actors.

I didn't want to be near any of it. In fact, with my son here, I knew I wanted a little space from NXIVM . . . but they wouldn't make it easy. Unfortunately, neither would my husband.

Around the time our child turned a year old, Nippy began to remind me how far we were from his family. Now that our son was getting more mobile, Nippy felt that it might be more beneficial for our careers and our young family if we moved to the East Coast, specifically New York. If we moved to Albany, he said, we could have a built-in community of friends and colleagues in NXIVM to help us out with baby-sitting while also being within a few hours of the city to go on auditions, line up work, and visit his parents when they were at their apartment in Manhattan. I really didn't want to move and leave my family, the center, or my community, but I wanted Nippy to feel supported in what he was asking me for.

By now it was clear that Barb J.'s death was one of the biggest losses of my life. Through the hard times, when I wasn't getting promoted and didn't think I could push through, she had always given me the strength to believe in myself and keep working. She was my coach, my confidante, my go-to within the organization. She'd never made me feel like I had to act or do anything differently in order to keep growing. She honored me just the way I was. I loved her so much.

And when it came to conversations about relocating to Albany, something else made me feel uncomfortable. On one occasion for a coach summit, a group of coaches from my center flew to Albany because we'd been told that Nancy would be teaching the coaching classes herself. When my team and I arrived in Albany only to discover that Nancy wasn't even there, we learned our responsibility for the summit would be to spend hours drafting letters to inform those who hadn't come how much their absence affected our team.

I was so pissed off. I had brought my staff there thinking that they would be receiving a rock star coaching training. When we got back to Vancouver, one of my coaches who had attended the summit dropped off the Stripe Path because she was so disappointed with the fact that the summit wasn't what we'd been promised. I tried sharing this feedback with the executive board, only to be told that this coach was clearly "entitled."

Throughout 2015, I continued to fly to Albany to attend "green meetings" as part of the highest ranks—however, I'd come to recognize that I still wasn't part of the inner circle. Even when I'd made it, I wasn't *really* one of them. Pam, Nancy, Lauren, all the executives, would continue to have conversations without including me. I never fully understood the chasm. I would piece together later that I was experiencing their resentment, as I had been able to glean all of the good from ESP, while they were literally slaves to Keith. When I was visiting Albany it was as if I was walking freely in their prison. They would go on to make decisions without getting my input about their potential impact on the students at the Vancouver center. I later found out that my elevation to green sash was simply a "motivational promotion," an attempt to make me feel inspired again so I'd stick around after my son was born and continue to recruit new paid members. It worked, and I was committed . . . until I wasn't.

Keith was working to develop new incentives to keep the average student motivated to bring in "fresh blood" (as Clare callously referred to new students). He introduced a points system, just like you get with your credit card or in coffee shops: *Buy nine and get the tenth free!* The idea as he pitched it was that we could use these points to receive future trainings at no cost. For example, if you referred someone to the Five-Day, whose price tag was now $2,400, then you would earn $240 worth of future curriculum.

The problem was that even I, one of the top salespeople in the company, enrolled only three people per year, max, into a Sixteen-Day, which was a minimum of $6,000. Most people did the Five-Day and sometimes continued with the following eleven, but rarely purchased the entire Sixteen-Day at once. With my friend and fellow field trainer Henry, I did the math. We figured out that you'd have to enroll between ten and seventeen people in a Sixteen-Day training to get one Level II training for free. You couldn't put any points toward a discount—you either sold so much that you got the training totally free, or you got nothing. To top it all off, the points expired in a year. The design of the system ensured you'd never get that discount.

Henry, who had degrees from Stanford and Harvard universities, inquired about the fact that the math didn't work out. "Can we just talk about these numbers?" he asked Keith in a field trainer meeting about the points incentive program. Henry spent the next twelve months filling out breach forms for having called out Keith in front of the senior leadership team.

Henry and I stayed in because we trusted the program and that Keith knew something we didn't see or understand. But as 2016 neared its close, there was an inner conflict brewing. Increasingly I was starting to see the bullshit for myself. Inside, I wanted to step back and focus on motherhood. I was conflicted because I felt that the senior executives in NXIVM were pushing me to commit even more. If we moved to Albany, the organization would be our life. I, who had once been so contagiously committed, wasn't on board. For so long, I'd considered myself an ESP "lifer," but in my heart I'd always known that I wanted to stay away from Albany. My husband was ready to leave Vancouver to get back to the East Coast, but I didn't want to give up what I had built. I wanted to grow but was feeling impatient with the tedious new trainings, which didn't ring true for me. I'd gotten involved with NXIVM because I wanted to discover my potential . . . and here, right at home, I'd found it. With Barb J. gone, no one had my back when Nancy subtly suggested that family would just cover my Inner Deficiency. What was limiting my happiness most of all was now NXIVM itself.

How would my feelings affect my marriage? What came next would make the answer very clear.

CHAPTER TWELVE

ILLUSION OF HOPE

NOVEMBER 2016–MARCH 2017

Just months after Barb Jeske died, we learned that Pam Cafritz was also terminally ill. This was insane—Pam had *just* given me my green sash. I wondered: Was there something in the water in Albany? I worried that a chemical in the area where they all lived was starting to make them all sick. Something definitely seemed toxic. Nancy had recently sustained a bout with breast cancer, and five other women in the community had also received grave diagnoses. Pam had been the picture of good health. She was fit, she'd been vegetarian for decades, and she had enough energy to keep up with Keith's new ideas. Pam had been Keith's go-to for everything, and while I observed that she wasn't always the most organized individual, I couldn't blame her. It would have been tough for anyone to be on their toes no matter what the hour to deliver whatever Keith asked for.

Two doctors who were part of the NXIVM community were overseeing Pam's treatment for renal cancer, but it had advanced too rapidly for them to gain control of. In November 2016, two years after Barb died, Pam Cafritz died, too.

It struck me as odd that Keith had given a directive to hold off on planning her funeral until January. So many of us had worked closely with Pam, and Nippy and I were tempted to book a flight to Albany— but it was too late to say goodbye. What was even weirder than waiting two months after Pam's death to hold the funeral was Keith and

Nancy's order to all of us senior-level coaches not to tell anyone that Pam had died. *What?!* Had anyone called her family? What the hell was going on?

Lauren explained it matter-of-factly: they were holding off on having the funeral until the annual coach summit, which was strongly recommended for every coach from all the centers to attend.

So in early January we traveled to the Albany area for Pam's funeral. From what I was told, they'd planned the event as a celebration, held at an exclusive wedding venue in the resort city of Saratoga Springs, near Albany. As we entered, we passed through floor-to-ceiling columns to explore the shadow box displays of Pam's belongings, the inner circle running around like headless chickens trying to put finishing touches on the decor even as the employees of the facility were directing us to take our seats. Over the years I'd realized that NXIVM events had always been like this: nothing started on time, and nothing was organized. The way my center ran was symbolic of the reason I wanted to stay in Vancouver: there, things operated smoothly. In Albany, there was always chaos. In a way, the scene at Pam's funeral was appropriate because she'd always been one of the first people tasked with trying to pull off whatever crazy vision Keith had. The reason for this emerged in a new light at the funeral, as I learned something about their relationship that I'd never known before. We'd always been told that Keith had no lovers . . . but at the funeral, Allison Mack took the microphone and assumed the role of emcee—that's right, an emcee at a funeral. As she spoke, she referred to Pam as Keith's "life partner."

Life partner?

I'd always thought of Pam as Keith's personal assistant. Had I heard that right? In the context of our surroundings, it started to make sense: Keith had called for this elaborate funeral production for the woman he loved. Was that it?

So maybe he did have a girlfriend, I thought. *But what's the big deal?* In two years, we'd lost two of our most integral leaders of more than a decade. I wasn't focused on the details of Keith's personal life as much as I was trying to comprehend how both of these women had died in such a similar way and thinking of the five other women in the organization who had gotten sick.

As Allison continued to talk about Pam's life before the funeral guests, I realized she spoke with a certain license—as if she'd now replaced Pam as Keith's number one. While Allison beamed in the spotlight, a few of the other coaches scrambled to play the slideshow they'd made in remembrance of Pam.

After a PowerPoint presentation of Pam's life in photos, the senior levels handed out headphone sets to us attendees as though we were in a museum. Nippy and I shared a glance as they encouraged us to explore the exhibit they'd produced in homage to Pam's life. Were they serious? I felt like we'd just arrived to tour Graceland.

For one of the stations, they'd actually put Pam's old athletic wear on mannequins. There, you'd stand and listen to the presentation in your headset about Pam's running career. They had exhibits like this for each aspect of her life, from her work in Jness to her humor, her legacy, and her favorite hobbies. It was the weirdest thing I'd ever seen, and I wondered: where was Pam's family? The choice of venue for dinner following the two-day funeral extravaganza was the most disjointed detail of all: NXIVM was supposed to be a vegetarian community, but the restaurant they'd rented out was at a famous Saratoga Springs steakhouse. The menu? A pasta buffet. Nothing about it was cohesive or genuinely representative of Pam.

Pam Cafritz's funeral was another thread that would unravel to reveal the earliest truth. The only way I can explain it now is that I have to wonder whether Keith produced this epic funeral either out of guilt or to make it look as though he had always been faithful to her. Perhaps the real motive behind this celebration of Pam's life was that Keith was ramping up hardcore for complete control. He was moving away from his older, longtime partners and just minutes away from launching his new initiative with the newer, younger women.

Just a few weeks after Pam's funeral, Lauren Salzman flew to Vancouver to visit me and to train a Five-Day. I was surprised when, for the first time ever, she wanted to stay at our place instead of a hotel. Right away I could tell something big was in the works. As soon as I picked her up she told me she had to talk to me about something. *Oh no . . . feedback from Lauren,* I thought. Greens had to be open to feedback at all times. I braced myself.

In my apartment one night while Nippy was at the gym, Lauren asked me, "How committed are you to your growth?"

"Very," I said. "I'm a green, right?"

She paused and took a breath. Then, almost mischievously, she said, "And what are you willing to do to grow?"

"Whatever it takes, obviously!" I said naively.

"OK," she told me. "It's a little weird, *but*—I want to invite you to something so amazing, it's life-changing. But it's top-secret, and before I can tell you anything, I need you to give me collateral to ensure that you won't tell anyone about it."

While I had never really given any serious collateral myself since the concept had been introduced, it had become a common practice within the community. Others had put money on the line if they failed to enroll enough students for an upcoming intensive, for example, but I had always thought this was a little extreme for a personal growth company. I'd managed to dodge losing anything of significance.

"I need to think about that," I said. My stomach dropped at the thought of giving her collateral just to hear more . . . but she looked so excited and I trusted her so much that I was also intrigued.

The next morning when we were both awake, Lauren asked me: "So, have you thought about it? Do you have any questions?" By the way she looked at her phone, I could always tell when she was texting with a higher rank. She was on me about this, and I could tell someone was on her. She was persistent, a little reminiscent of Suzanne on that first cruise back in 2005.

I had thought about it, but, *collateral* . . . just to hear about this thing? That sounded a bit much. I've never had many secrets; I've always been a pretty open book. It took me a good day to come up with something private that I thought might be really revealing, how I'd done some recreational drugs in high school. "Here," Lauren said.

"Write it down." As she took a photo of what I'd written and then tex-ted it to someone else, I could see she'd organized quite a system for acceptance into this new program. *Who had she sent that to?*

A moment later, she glanced at her phone for a pause and then looked back at me. "That's not damaging enough. Do it again, just make it worse."

Alright, they wanted me to dig deeper . . . but I was struggling. I wrote down something about a fling I had years ago that I would have preferred to keep private.

Lauren looked at it. "Worse."

Seeing that I was at a loss for ideas, she muttered, "Just make it up."

I looked at what I'd written the first time, and exaggerated it, fab-ricating details. Again, Lauren took a picture with her phone and sent the photo off. A moment later, after I noticed her glance down at her phone again, I figured that had been acceptable—because next, she gave me the lift. "OK," she said. "I want to invite you to a top secret international women's group—*just* for women—to change the world." She called this program "DOS."

"*Doss?*" I asked her.

Lauren let me in on it: she was part of an elite women's group, she said, that was designed to be a practical, advanced program where a select circle of women would commit fully to live our lives by some of the concepts like we'd learned in Jness. It was its own aggressive track with some from the NXIVM community and some from outside, and not everybody in ESP would be invited or could even know about it—not a word. Joining would require a lifelong pledge to the group and this "collateral" to cement the promise of utmost secrecy. "Can I tell Nippy?"

"No," she said. "He doesn't need to know. It's a private choice you're making about your growth that will help your relationship overall."

I tried to imagine locking myself into anything without dis-cussing it with my husband first . . . but we had been disagreeing about where to live, and I thought this might help smooth out the bumps in our relationship. Maybe this was what I'd been needing—a higher-level system within the community to present me with something new that would pull me forward with its challenges. With a group of other young women? This could be inspiring. So much had happened in the twelve years since I got in, especially since we'd lost Pam and Barb. Lauren was right: we needed something specifically targeted at us young women. The men's group had bonded so tightly. Besides, I had stagnated on the Stripe Path and was itching for more growth and to make more of a difference in the world.

It sounded amazing, but now Lauren said my collateral wasn't strong enough. She suggested I submit a nude photo. *What?* I felt a flutter of nerves in my stomach, but I couldn't be a chicken about posing naked. She told me she did it herself and found it empowering. From what Lauren said, DOS was my chance to be part of this strong, spiritual club of women. If I accepted, this would be a lifelong commitment and would be run by us, for us. I liked the idea of having some of these women in my life forever—they were my friends, and that was my intention anyway. But how many groups of friends get to enter into an agreement together to stand with one another as we each work to become the most powerful versions of ourselves? Lauren promised that this would help me reach my goals, and we would be part of a hand-selected group of women who would change the world. Later when I told Nippy that I would be "embarking on a new growth push with my fellow greens" as Lauren had guided me to say, he was nonchalant. "Cool," he said.

Lauren said that the photo needed to show both my face as well as my privates. It would certainly prove to be my most limber photo shoot, as I posed before a full-length mirror contorting myself to capture the whole thing with her phone while making sure to get a clear image of my face, as Lauren had instructed. It's what I'd say anytime a couple of us were out shopping together or changing into our costumes for our tribute presentation at V-Week: "We all have the same parts, right?" If we were entering a sacred group together as women, then what was more sacred than embracing our bodies and documenting them in a photo?

Then I got the details. "The first step is making a lifetime vow of obedience."

"Obedience" was a word we'd used throughout Jness—a term that always made me roll my eyes. Keith had taught us about Ghandi's wife and how she had served him so that he could do his life's work. It's just an exercise, Lauren had said, and we lived so far apart. How bad could it really be for me to make a vow of obedience? "Alright," I said with a shrug.

"It's a lifetime commitment to me," she said. I was already committed to her. That was easy.

The second point was that I had to agree that I would be Lauren's slave, and she'd be my master. I must have given her an incredulous look, because she quickly explained further. "Not like a *real* slave," she said flippantly. "It's not like you're going to live inside a cage or anything." Well *that* was reassuring. "It's just an exercise. Think of it like a heightened coaching relationship."

The third thing I had to agree to was to wear a piece of jewelry, like a necklace, anklet, or chain around my belly, that I would never take off, to symbolize the chain to one's master. Lauren said I could take my time choosing the perfect piece.

The final commitment was the tattoo, as she called it at the time. She told me it was the size of dime and it would be really pretty.

But this was my biggest sticking point. I told her I had never gotten a tattoo for a number of personal reasons. She understood, she said, and she would help me get through that with some EMs. She said that the initiation ceremony wouldn't be until my next visit to Albany, so it wasn't happening right away.

If it seems like I should have wielded more suspicion as I entered into this, it's important to understand the way I saw it at the time: Lauren Salzman was one of the people I trusted most, the godmother of my child. She was also pretty much as high up as it got in the company, and here she was, in my home, offering to take me on and mentor me. For life.

I'd also taken a vow of obedience. I decided just to go with it. My collateral was on the line, and what could have gotten released wasn't even truly representative of me.

On the last day of that Five-Day training, I happened to catch a little gesture out of the corner of my eye. One of my lower ranking staff members, a proctor from the West Coast, exited the proctor office and tugged on her underwear line, wincing slightly in pain. "Are you ok?" I asked.

"Oh yeah," she said. "It's just a little cut."

It was bizarre, and I clocked it. The area that seemed painful was the same place Lauren had pointed to on her pelvis when she had told me about the tattoo. *Oh,* I thought, *if she is in this thing*—someone who was of lower rank and far less committed than I perceived myself to be—*then why not?* I told Lauren I was in.

But the collateral I had given wasn't enough. Lauren said I need to fully collateralize my whole life. That I had to put everything on the line so that I would never leave. I remember thinking that was a little sneaky. I'd given a nude photo, and it was hard to turn back now. What else could I submit? I didn't have any dark secrets. On the last day of her stay with me, Lauren instructed me to record four videos: one saying something untrue about my husband, another doing the same about my mom, one about my dad, and the last about my half-brother. She sat in the passenger's seat in my car while I spoke and pretended not to know I was being videotaped. The idea was to make it look candid, because who would ever record themselves saying such awful things? I used my best acting to reveal things about my loved ones that weren't even true, including that Nippy sometimes gets so angry that he's violent and abusive. In truth, that had never happened. He has never hit me or touched me in a way that was unloving.

All of these videos were designed to damage my relationships and hurt the reputations of my loved ones if released.

The whole time, I had so many questions. "Who else is in this group?" I asked.

"You don't need to know. You need to submit to this process. It will help you get over your control issues more than anything else you've done."

"Does Keith know about this?"

"No, it's a women's-only group!"

I feel stupid now, having believed her. The women in Albany often consulted Keith in their decision-making. I recall asking Allison Mack to attend our wedding back in 2013, and she told me she had to ask Keith first if she could leave town. *What?* I thought to myself. *How old are you? Is Keith your dad?* I'd kept my judgment silent.

"What should I tell Nippy about this?" I asked Lauren.

She advised me to tell him that the greens were going to be pushing me on growth. "Tell him you might be doing some things that don't make sense," she said, "but just ask him to be supportive."

After she went home, Lauren texted me with a reminder that I wasn't "fully collateralized" yet. I was supposed to put more on the line to know I would "blow up my life" if I strayed from the path. *Collaterals should be taken into consideration,* she said. *Work, family, social credibility, important people, assets, wealth, rights, possessions.* OK, but . . . I thought it was just an exercise. This made it sound a little more serious. For sure this was just part of the setup, right?

From a distance, our new relationship began. Her first assignment for me was to help me with Nippy. "Spend one day when you don't ask him for anything," she suggested. "Don't ask him to do anything for you, don't ask for anything you want to borrow, don't engage with him on any level where you're depending on him." It felt like a relatively normal exchange within NXIVM . . . except that I was calling my best friend Master.

We were also supposed to practice daily acts of denial, like not eating sugar or drinking caffeine, or taking a cold shower. This was pretty typical of our usual penances, and I've always been a relatively healthy eater so to avoid sugar or stick to herbal teas was not a major sacrifice for me. But we also had to do an hour of work per week for our master—for the purpose, she said, of moving our attention away from ourselves and focusing on "other." The premise as she explained it was that learning to put another individual first was the ultimate act of spirituality. Anybody on the planet who had a child or significant other could agree with this—I'd learned how amazing it felt to put my child or anyone I loved deeply before myself. Lauren called this hour of service per week as part of the slave-master arrangement the "weekly act of care."

From a distance, I couldn't do a ton for her, so mainly I filled her Level II trainings or coached her duckies on enrollment skills. I knew that was helpful because it brought her income. I also worked with her assistant, whom she'd been having trouble with, giving the young woman tools to be more proactive and efficient. These were things I had learned from successes and failures with my assistants over the years. Once, before I flew to Albany, I bought Lauren a few bags of her favorite kind of granola from the juice shop in my neighborhood. My acts of care for her were all pretty easy—things I enjoyed doing for her anyway.

She instructed me to respond to daily "readiness drills." For three years we'd been doing this as an exercise that Keith had designed to strengthen teamwork in SOP. If anyone in the group didn't respond to the drill, it would be the job of someone in the team to go looking for them. When Lauren would text me with the question mark *?* for the word "Ready?" at any hour of the day or night, I'd have sixty seconds to respond *R* for "I'm ready." If we failed to respond, we could expect to be punished, possibly with the release of our collateral.

I was already sleep-deprived from having a toddler, and with the three-hour time difference between Albany and Vancouver, most of the drills occurred between 3 A.M. and 6 A.M. on my end. Occasionally Nippy would stir in bed when my phone lit up, and I'd duck out of the room, so he'd think I was going to change a diaper. Lauren expected me to answer if I was sleeping, if I was driving, if I was in bed with Nippy, if I was visiting one of my parents with my son. Even if I was in yoga class, Lauren wanted me to hide my phone under my mat and text *R* quickly. I'd gone to my yoga studio for years and wasn't going to risk being kicked out if my instructor caught me texting in class. From my child's safety to my wellness practice and my marriage, nothing was allowed to be more sacred than being reachable for the readiness drills. You could only be dark if you were leaving cell service or on an airplane. The demands were driving me mad. Every time I got into the elevator in my building, I'd have to text *Dark. Elevator.*

When I exited seconds later, I texted, *Undark.*

When I got into my car, I texted, *Dark. Driving.*

It occupied so much of my focus, that after a couple of weeks, I realized it was starting to consume me. The sleep deprivation, the incessant checking of my phone, the juggling between attending to my child and rushing to respond—because if I didn't, I'd be in trouble. Nippy was used to my taking coaching texts and calls, but it was getting out of control. I finally told Lauren, "I'm not going to text you anymore while I'm driving." There was no way I'd take the chance of getting in an accident with my son in the car. I could feel the dissatisfaction in her lack of response to me.

Collaterals should be taken into consideration. On occasion I scrolled up to look at that text from several weeks ago. Now I could discern the tone in which she'd made that statement: she wasn't playing around. She was reminding me what was at stake if I didn't obey. For years I had opened my heart to Lauren about some of the most personal parts of my life. She didn't need to threaten my relationships or my reputation to get me to do whatever she asked. Why was she taking this so far? Was this really Lauren's idea, or had someone put her up to it?

Every new ask from her made me wonder what I'd gotten myself into, and the "slave-master" thing was starting to feel literal as she was starting to speak and text with me like she was talking down to me— not like she was being a loving mentor as she originally promised. I was not allowed to be inaccessible, but if Lauren had to go dark, another master would sub in for her and text me. The number was never one I recognized, and I never got a text from the same number twice. All this made it clear that whoever texted me when Lauren was dark was using a burner phone. Anytime I stated my concern, Lauren would contact me to let me know her sister in her DOS circle had reported that I'd been arrogant and entitled. "How so?" I said. "I was ready."

"You're doing it now. See?"

"But I'm trying to be better. Tell me, what did I do?"

"You need to figure it out and come back to me. You have already taken enough of my time. What does it mean that now you want more by asking me to tell you how you failed? Figure it out."

Lauren had always been so kind, so relatable. But I noticed that as soon as we entered into this relationship, she turned extremely condescending toward me. Our relationship suddenly felt very hierarchical, and at times when I could tell she was aware she was coming off as visibly harsh, she would remind me that this was for my benefit and it was a privilege for me to be part of this. While she said my being her slave was only an exercise, there was definitely a dynamic in our relationship that made it clear she was superior. She was being *kind* of a bitch. But that was like . . . *part* of it, right?

She was waiting for me to fulfill another requirement, which was to recruit six of my own slaves to become a grandmaster. "*Six?*" I asked. A grandmaster—what was this, the Ku Klux Klan? When I didn't show immediate enthusiasm to scout my own slaves, Lauren repositioned the idea to me. "Imagine having six people doing an hour of work for you a week," she said. "Think of the money you'll save, and how you'll be leveraging your time." Still, I was so unsure. When I needed an extra hand with an errand or help around the house, Nippy or one of my parents was always available. I also had paid for regular cleanings and paid my assistant far above the going rates. I remembered what it was like in the early days in the community when I'd worked for free. I couldn't imagine asking someone to work for nothing, doing personal favors for me.

"Think of who you want to have a lifetime commitment with." The first person I thought of was Paige, one of my closest friends from Vancouver who had been in my *Artist's Way* group and had been doing ESP with me since the beginning. Lauren informed me: "You can't have her." She was asking us to commit ourselves to this calling for life, but she was treating it like a game—a game that only she knew the rules to. I didn't want to *have* anyone—Lauren was making it sound like owning someone had been my objective.

How many layers of this operation were there—meaning, how had they already gotten in contact with some of the women from the

Vancouver center? I *hated* when anyone tried to poach someone from within my line; that was totally and clearly against the organization's written standards from the time you applied to be a coach. It was actually in the coaching contract that we weren't allowed to recruit ESP members into any other business, club, or program. How long had this been going on?

There was another young woman from our center who was dear to me. Susanna had changed careers after she started coming to Ethos, and now she was killing it with a really awesome business idea she'd developed. She was dedicated to the program and had recently become a coach. She was beautiful, sweet, and humble, and had a genuineness about her that I really appreciated. We loved to meet for dinner at the vegetarian restaurant in my neighborhood. The thing was, we'd only known each other for a couple of years. I didn't want to have a lifetime commitment to someone I wasn't very close to, nor did I know what she would think of my asking this of her. "I think she'd be perfect," Lauren said, prompting me to reach out to Susanna.

Reluctantly, I followed Lauren's guidance and invited Susanna over for tea, to check in on how she was doing with her life and on the Stripe Path. I did the first step of the DOS pitch with her, as Lauren did with me. Susanna had just come back from doing the Jness track in Mexico City and was totally primed to be invited to a secret group for women, I thought. So when I told her about collateral, it didn't take long for her to make a "candid" video—she was dying to know what the big secret was!

I texted Lauren the video and was about to do the full pitch, but she freaked out over text and told me not to continue. Apparently another sister in her circle had a slave, like me, who wanted to enroll Susanna in DOS herself.

What? What is going on here? I didn't know who all the players were, but I never made the four-point pitch (lifetime vow of obedience, master/slave, necklace, and tattoo) to Susanna, because Lauren explained that I had jumped the gun. If there were two masters "vested" in a potential new recruit, the slave should receive the pitch from a non-biased party. In this case, someone else from Lauren's circle was going to have to pitch her now. She told me to tell Susanna that someone would be calling to give her the full lowdown, and then she could choose between me, or this other person, to be her master.

Lauren emphasized how important it was that the pitch was clear and delivered just-so to a new recruit for DOS. Lauren told the girl that she wasn't supposed to tell anyone who gave her the pitch. Shortly after, Lauren texted me, saying, *Congratulations, Susanna chose you.* Days later, Susanna let it slip: "When Alli told me what it was all about, I wasn't really sure, but then I couldn't say no!—," she said, before catching herself. "Oh shit," she said. "I forgot I wasn't supposed to tell you who made the pitch to me." This was when I knew that Allison Mack was involved in DOS. I'd thought as much, because Allison had become close friends with Nicki and some of the other women who had picked up and settled down in Albany. It seemed fitting that they would all make lifetime commitments to each other.

So now I had one slave. The whole thing was weird but also kind of fun at first—our own secret club! Lauren suggested another woman to me who was also very pretty. Now that I know who some of the other young women in DOS were, it's so clear from my years in NXIVM to see that Keith went for certain types: long hair, extremely skinny, snapshots of the 1970s. He shunned women who were a little bigger and didn't include them as part of the community.

When the truth about DOS later exploded, it was said he even asked the women he slept with not to trim their pubic hair to retain the pheromones. It was deep control—these women did what he liked. I even remember how in the early days of ESP, all the women who lived in Albany said they had a garlic allergy. I thought this was so strange, until I learned years later that when you eat garlic, it can make your vagina take on the same scent. (Women who more recently have revealed to me that they had relationships with Keith said he couldn't always perform, but he absolutely loved giving oral sex to women. That was known to be his "thing.")

Lauren texted me daily to ensure I followed through on recruiting another slave. Finally, after weeks of stalling and waiting for the "right moment" where I'd established a good rapport and trust with the woman, I did the pitch. She said no. "OK! I understand," I responded. I was so relieved. I hadn't even wanted to take her on—to coach her for the rest of her life? I really liked her, but I barely knew her! I was planning on being in ESP for the rest of my life and now I was committed to DOS. Taking this young woman on would have been like marrying someone after a few dates. It was just a little too soon.

When I reported back to Lauren that she'd declined the pitch, Lauren told me I couldn't let her off the hook so easily and demanded I set up a three way call. After the two of us spent three hours with her on the phone the DOS prospect agreed to "think on it."

In that torturous phone call I started to learn the pitch that Lauren and her DOS sisters were using (and took notes):

> True commitment to any one thing is commitment to every-thing . . . in our lives, as women, we always have a back door. Keeping the back door open gives us the wiggle room to never have character, to never have discipline or follow-through, to never have a full sense of self or self-esteem.

> We need to learn commitment and there's no place in society to get it because we can get out of everything. Most women never have an "all-in" commitment in their entire life.

I could see that it would be much easier for them to recruit women who had been through the Jness curriculum, as they were more prone to joining a sisterhood of empowered women.

So now I had one slave and one pending, neither of which I had recruited by myself. The third would be a lovely Ethos student who was also in Jness so she too understood the concepts I was laying out. She said yes immediately, but that relationship only lasted a few weeks before I decided to blow it up.

Thankfully, I never made it to Grandmaster, or even found out what that even meant. But *my* Master, always with a capital M as she had ordered, was not letting me off the hook with pulling in new recruits. She'd given the order that I was to communicate with her about DOS only using Telegram, a Russian messenger app where texts were encrypted and could be set to self-destruct once complete. Whenever I put my child in his high chair or down for a nap long enough to look at my phone, a series of text messages from Lauren looked like this:

Check private thread   11:45AM
Check thread   11:54AM
Check thread   12:01PM
See thread   12:23PM

She was insistent, incessant. I hurried over to the private thread, where she was pressing hard to know if that second recruit had committed. *She still has more questions,* I said. *Please send me a video chat when You have a sec.*

Yes, I was to capitalize the word You anytime I was in a written conversation with her. *Mimi and I are both ready!* she responded, sending a selfie of her holding her hairless cat.

I miss You! I'd say in response. *Can't wait to see You! Would love to get You back here soon!*

While I pretended to be all-in, the prospective recruit voiced her aversion to the slave-master concept over text, asking about:

1. committing to a situation for my life with lack of data of what's involved now and in the future

2. being someone's "s." Not trusting their intentions or that they know what's best for me. Giving up ownership of my life. Saying someone else is the boss of my life and how weak that makes me feel.

Obviously two very valid questions. Lauren's response? A thumbs-up emoji. That was it, like "Oh, we've got this." She didn't care at all about this woman's concerns. A half hour later Lauren pinged me with *Want to recap?*

I told her I would love to but was just about to feed my son dinner. *What's your evening like?* I asked.

I am going into a meeting now. I can message when done.

A meeting? It was 5:53 P.M. my time, going on 9 P.M. Albany time. Still, as I tried to feed our son while Nippy prepared dinner, the simplest response was to play along. *Perfect!*

Twenty minutes later, she messaged me. *Ok free.*

That message had come in at 6:11 P.M., and I was supposed to be available at all times for my "Master." When I didn't message back until 6:13, I apologized profusely. *I'm so sorry! It's chaos here. Can I have 20 more minutes?*

I may sleep but text me to see . . .

She was threatening to go dark on me. My stomach dropped. One minute late on grabbing my phone, and I'd failed.

Then I got a message from the new recruit: *So if I wanna do it what's the next step?*

Oh God. I didn't know, so I passed the question onto Lauren.

The next step is she commits and we go forward. Is she saying she's IN? Lauren asked, continuing, *I might say, "I don't know . . . are you saying you want to do it??"*

Copy! I said—and five minutes later, at 6:23 P.M., I sent Lauren a follow-up text. *She is in!!!!!*

BOOM! she wrote. *I'M SO EXCITED!!!! CONGRATULATIONS!!!*

We'd begun exchanging the emoji of two intertwined chain links to celebrate our membership in this club—symbolizing, obviously, our participation in the slave-master group. *Good morning Master!* I was now texting to Lauren in the mornings, with a kiss, a heart, and the chain link emoji. *Good night Master!* 🌙🖤🔗 I saluted at the end of the day, using the same three symbols. I was trying to think of the word Master more like teacher, or maybe coach. In the beginning, she'd said the term was nothing more than a formality. But she never told me to drop it, which by now I had to admit I was hoping she'd do.

Nothing about these discussions sat easily with me. What did I *think* the chain links suggested? While the slave arrangement played out, I would sometimes recall Lauren's comment from the day she first approached me about DOS: *It's not like you're going to live in a cage or anything.* At the time I believed there was no real cage, and there were no real shackles . . . but with that collateral, I never for one second forgot that I was bound.

If Lauren knew back then what my relationships with my own two slaves were like, I'm sure she'd have said I was too soft. I did the readiness drills but didn't punish the women in my line if it took them more than a minute to respond to me. I didn't push the weekly "act of care" or insist that they do an hour of work for me per week because I thought it was unfair. Most bizarre of all was hearing the girls call me Master, and each time, I wanted to tell them to stop. Why were we doing this? Lauren explained to me that we were using the drills with our slaves to "build the muscle of readiness." This was classic behavioral stimulus-response training, and frankly, looking back, it had Keith's influence written all over it. By participating in the readiness drills, Lauren was training her slaves, and I was training mine, to do what we said the minute we said it. This was all a buildup to the main point of DOS. The initials stood for *dominus obsequious sororium*, Latin for "master over the slave women."

Susanna sent me her full collateral to finalize her commitment, and my eyes went wide at how faithfully she'd embraced the task when I watched just a few seconds of a video where she'd danced naked before the camera. She trusted me. I could not ask her, or any of my "slaves," to do me favors or call me Master. More than anything, I had joined this secret society of women out of my desire to continue my growth. Therefore, I would provide for my slaves the service that I'd hoped Lauren would provide for me when I agreed to get into DOS. I made it my job to coach them.

That March, just a few weeks after Lauren had come to stay with me to pull me into DOS, I flew to Albany for what Lauren had called an "initiation ceremony" that she'd be leading. She said we'd all be getting a matching dime-size tattoo, a beautiful design. This part—the tattoo—still made me nervous, but if it was the size of a dime and we were all getting it together . . . Lauren said that by the end of the initiation ritual, my life would be changed. The ceremony would take place on March 9, 2017.

When I got to Albany, I couldn't shake my unease. I didn't want a tattoo. "I don't want anything on my body," I told Lauren.

She responded with the classic NXIVM flip. "What do you make it mean?"

"My body is clean," I told her. "I've never wanted to have any marks on it."

"But what if," she said, "what if it stands for your character and your strength as symbolized on your body?"

My body had always been pure. I treat it with such care: what I feed myself, my daily exercise, rarely drinking alcohol, vitamins, hot lemon water packed in a travel mug, and sufficient sleep (until motherhood and this slave-master thing began to call me out of bed at all hours). I was thankful that I've never been seriously injured or required surgery that would have produced any scars. For my whole life, I was healthy.

But on the afternoon of March 9, 2017, I submitted my body to another force. I lay on that exam table with a professional licensed physician standing over me. Did I want to go through with it? No, not at all . . . but my collateral had a lot of power. Inside that room as we took turns lying on the table, there was never a moment when I didn't feel self-conscious about being unclothed. I bared all of myself for this organization in both the literal and the figurative sense. The feeling in the room was not one of unconditional acceptance or female empowerment. With Lauren overseeing everything, I felt judged. I couldn't shed it: you think of that one freckle on your butt that you sometimes catch in the mirror, the stretch marks from having lost weight or borne a child, the bikini line you wish you'd taken the time to groom. I had entered into this rite out of love for Lauren and a desire to grow, but from the beginning of this initiative with DOS, Lauren had not shown love in return. As she stood back with a smile on her face while she filmed each branding, the mood was not one of loving support, but rather watchfulness. Power. Dominance over submissives, under the guise of a supportive sisterhood. When I lay down on that table, I handed over my most important possession, my well-being, into someone else's hands—whose, I wasn't even totally sure.

■ ■ ■

That night when one of my sisters dropped me off back at our condo, I stuck closely to Lauren's instructions. I acted as if we'd just been at a day-long meeting for greens.

But when we reached our condo, I stepped into the bathroom and examined my burn. Danielle had put an antibacterial ointment over it, and the area still stung. A very faint burning smell also lingered. I covered it back up and slipped into pajamas and pretended that all was well. Still partly disassociated, I lay in bed for hours unable to sleep.

The next morning, I was still haunted. NXIVM had become a deeper part of me—now, in the physical sense—than I had ever wanted. I knew that if I tried to voice any of this, they'd say I had no character, no honor, that I was a complainer, a parasite throwing a tantrum. They'd say that my behavior was exactly the reason that a group like DOS needed to exist, because women who get uncomfortable and indulge their discomfort are weak. "Go as long as you can without letting Nippy see this," Lauren said, gesturing to my mark. "You have to make sure he doesn't form a link between this and Albany."

I couldn't let Nippy find out. Over the past twelve years, the organization had disassembled my understanding of strength versus weakness. My dad had taught me that courage is not the absence of fear, but action despite fear. I'd been raised to voice the truth, to do the hard thing, to stand against what seemed to be wrong. But in NXIVM, through years of coaching, reinforcement of some behaviors and punishment for others, the senior levels had trained me to believe that staying silent was right.

The day after we'd gotten branded, our newly formed circle met with Lauren for lunch so that she could brief us on the logistics of communicating with each other. "I have to go," she said—but she requested that before we all left, we should form a line, standing buck naked, and set the timer on one of our iPhone cameras so we could capture the image of all of us posing nude as a group. Then she wanted us to send it to her.

Before we drove back to Apropos to attend the tenth eight-day Jness training and before one of the women left to fly home to California, we all stripped, took the photo, and sent it to Lauren. A while later she responded and said that we didn't look happy enough; that some of us looked bashful and a couple of us were covering our breasts. She ordered us to gather again and retake it.

I was back at our condo now. I'd just taken melatonin and couldn't drive a half hour back to Clifton Park. Another woman had already bought her train ticket to leave town. I told Lauren it was nearly impossible, and she said, "figure it out." We agreed that we'd get together the next morning before class and would all share the cost of buying our sister another ticket so that we could retake the photo, per our Master's request. Again, we sent it to Lauren. This time she let us know it was satisfactory.

As I look back at my texts to Lauren during those few weeks following the branding, I see that I stated everything with an exclamation point—as though beneath the words I was transmitting, a truth was fighting to come through. *Perfect!* I would say. *I can't wait to see You! Good morning Master!* Every exclamation point from that period of time was me trying to convince myself of something I didn't believe, and my desperation for Lauren to love me for who I really was instead of making me feel that I needed to improve or earn her consistent attention.

Before I flew home following the branding ceremony, Keith and Nancy had asked me to appear in a promo video as a spokesperson for the new point system they were offering. I agreed, reading over some notes on a teleprompter while a production crew in the mini production studio off Nancy's garage tested their equipment. I tried to stay upbeat and focus on the talking points they'd given me, but I felt fried. I was literally wounded.

I stepped into Nancy's kitchen to get caffeinated. There, I bumped into Keith, where he told me to just make sure I was in a good state.

"The main thing is that you're enthusiastic," he said, adding something that I'll never forget: "your job is to create the illusion of hope."

An illusion of hope? It hit me. To Keith, I was the actress who'd used NXIVM to go from the basement suite to a beautiful home. I had put in years of hard work, but to him, NXIVM wasn't a place for us to self-actualize; it was a strategy to gain money and power from other people. *The illusion of hope.* It was a fool's errand, all of it. The Stripe Path. The Mission. It was all phony.

That exchange in Nancy's kitchen, when he'd revealed the "illusion of hope," was the last time I would ever see Keith Raniere.

CHAPTER THIRTEEN

NONDISCLOSURE

MARCH–MAY 2017

As soon as I arrived home from Albany, Lauren informed me of the next step in finalizing my collateral: I would need to find a lawyer who would draw up a legal contract to put the deed for my home in her name.

So far I'd been successful at keeping the brand a secret, and in a way, it made me feel strong, like I'd won that part of the challenge. But changing the deed to our house felt impossible; beyond the scope of this now ridiculous game. I felt like a boulder had landed on my chest. My training kicked in and I remembered what the upper ranks had always said about this viscera: *That means you're doing it right.*

Lauren tried to assure me that this was just for her to hold in case I ever broke my word and commitment to myself and to DOS. But I was about to reach my tipping point. This was the first time I consciously allowed myself to examine what NXIVM's definition of "doing it right" was. Right for whom? Did Lauren actually think she could take our home from us?

"I don't know how to do that kind of legal transfer," I told her, and I didn't, but of course I could have figured it out if I wanted to. "I'll get on it," I said, promising to bring the paperwork when I came out east again in June for the next coach summit.

I got started searching—but not for a lawyer, for a way out. I wanted out of DOS, I wanted out of NXIVM, and I was so afraid that my husband, the person I could count on to always have my back, would still want us both to stay in. What would happen if I wanted out and he didn't? I had to go about all of this very, very carefully.

I needed time to think. For the first time during my tenure in NXIVM, I began to lie to my coach. I'd tell Lauren that I was going dark for a long audition or for a swim at our fitness center. I was so blissed out to have a small chunk of time with no readiness drills. I'd take my son to the park or walk him in his stroller around the farmers' market. I'd take a nice long nap. If I ran into somebody from the Vancouver Ethos center when I was out for an errand, I felt some buffer of reassurance that in Vancouver, I was the upline link to Lauren. The chances that I'd get busted for being dishonest were slim . . . though I remained conscious of what was at stake. To be honest, in some ways I just didn't take it too seriously, until I happened to watch an episode of a Netflix series where hackers had secretly recorded a teenage boy while he was masturbating to Internet porn and threatened to release the video as blackmail unless he did everything they said. He was coerced to respond to texts from an unknown number, completing dangerous assignments orchestrated by a stranger. It hit me how manipulative this whole charade was, and I really started questioning—who has my collateral? What if it got into the wrong hands?

I decided to treat it as business as usual until I could find a way out. I'd check in and tell Lauren that my slaves had done their act of service for me, when instead I'd used those hours in the week to work with them on their goals. As a circle, we had a daily quota to keep up with our enrollment. Also, every day we were reporting our numbers and who we had on our list. At this point, I called dibs and put everyone on my list whom I wanted to protect from being recruited by anyone else. I didn't want them to be branded and bound into what I had unwittingly committed to.

And then, the clincher: we had failed at the 3 A.M. readiness drills, and Lauren told one of our sisters to inform us that if we failed again, she was going to get paddled and locked inside a cage.

Oh my fucking word, I thought. *Are they serious?* A cage—was there a cage after all?

This was definitely a major turning point for me. Shit had just gotten even weirder, and kinky! One of the sisters in my circle had decided that if our Master was getting punished, then she thought that we should too. She asked her how many times Lauren had been paddled, and with what? My "sister" encouraged us all to do the same thing, and Lauren instructed her to purchase a paddle for us to use on each other, buck naked, and videotape it. Then we were to text it to her. The two women from California paddled each other, as did the sisters from Mexico. Lucky for me, I couldn't paddle myself in Vancouver. I promised I would have someone do it for me next time we were gathering in Albany for the next summit. But this was one of the final straws for me. I went along with it, over text, but was now frantically plotting my escape.

Meanwhile, as the brand stopped oozing pus and began to scab over, this all would grow much more serious. I'd begun to fantasize how I might go about writing an anonymous letter to Nancy to expose this fanatical offshoot of NXIVM. If she knew what was going on, then she needed to know that there was someone who was not OK with it. And if she didn't know, then she should have. But I didn't write the letter. I didn't know who was in on this, or how all the informed parties felt about it. I didn't know who I could talk to, nor who I could trust with my safety. If they were insane enough to mark our bodies with an iron and demand the title for my home, what else would they do?

Each morning after the branding ceremony when I woke up, I realized all over again that the mark on my body was forever. I stared at the ceiling with my head on the pillow as tears soaked my hair. I prayed that I could call Lauren and say: "You're never going to believe this, but I just had the strangest dream. You recruited me to a secret society of women, and we all had to get these weird brands on our bodies!" Then we'd laugh together at how silly that would be.

I knew that another branding session was scheduled in Albany a few weeks later for more women to join DOS at the annual summer coach summit; as a slave in Lauren's lineage, I would be expected to attend. She had recruited her sixth slave and was going to become a grandmaster. I couldn't let it happen, but I was sick with worry. What would the repercussions be? Would they publish my collateral? That would ruin my career and potentially my marriage. There was only one person left who was real enough to help me figure out what to do, and that was the friend who'd gotten me into this twelve years ago: Mark Vicente.

The previous January, Mark's wife, Bonnie, had made what had seemed like a sudden decision to leave NXIVM, and it was my job as the upline green sash in her lineage to see that she completed her exit paperwork (which included a gag order and a form stating that she had turned in all her materials and was leaving on good terms—essentially an exit NDA). When Bonnie didn't respond to me, I hoped that Lauren would let it rest. Instead, she insisted they needed Bonnie's signature affirming that she wouldn't ever share what she'd experienced during her time in the organization.

Lauren asked me to reach out to Mark, like a spy, to see if he knew what was going on. He'd been my business partner and my close friend for more than a decade, and he'd been as devoted to ESP and NXIVM as I had been if not more. Both of us had been avoiding having this long-overdue heart-to-heart. Neither knew whether the other was aware of all the weirdness that was going on.

When I finally got him on the phone, we discussed his wife's hesitation in filling out her exit paperwork. Mark told me that I'd sounded "manipulative" in the voicemail I'd left her—to which I got very defensive. I was just doing my job as her upline green. I didn't realize, at that time in early 2017, that my DOS duties were bleeding into NXIVM. Mark could tell I was loyal to Lauren in a way he didn't understand.

We didn't really talk further until Mark was in town to direct a web series Nippy was producing in mid-April. We were sitting in the car when he asked me pointedly, "How are you and Nippy doing?"

"Actually, we've been arguing lately," I said. "He wants to move to Albany, and I don't."

"God," Mark said. "Please don't move to Albany." I sat quietly for a second. As my sponsor, the person who had brought me in to the organization, Mark had always been the one who'd encouraged me to invest myself deeper with Keith, Nancy, and the team in Albany. This was a turning point. "There's something going on with the women there," he continued. "It's like some alternative Stripe Path, and Allison Mack is at the top."

Oh my God, I thought. *He knows.*

Mark continued. "Everyone's so thin, they're miserable, the upper ranks aren't even successful. There's something strange going on. I don't know what it is. Everyone is being really weird and secretive."

My first thought was that I had to tell Lauren. My programming to be loyal was a strong pull. I would get brownie points for being a good spy reporting back to her that Mark had a hint about DOS. But then I snapped back to reality and reconnected with my intuition, as the possibility occurred to me that Mark knew more than I did . . . and that maybe somehow he would provide a way out.

With my heart pounding, carefully, I initiated a low-key line of questioning. "So, if someone was in this said group . . . how would they get out of it?" I couldn't reveal to him that I wasn't asking for a friend. Not yet. I was too afraid of my collateral being released.

As our conversation continued it was as if we were both dancing around the truth . . . but with our conversation lingering in my mind, that night at home, I stood in front of the mirror and studied the brand. There, in the mirror, I saw it: the *A* and the *M*.

Holy shit. I had Allison Mack's initials on my fucking body.

To say I was enraged doesn't even touch my feelings. I *never* asked for this! I never consented to this! And I had no idea it was going to get worse.

Then, in mid-May, Mark gave me the heads-up that he was about to submit a resignation letter to the company. Something about this comforted me. I'd already decided that I wanted out, but I knew I was tied with my collateral. I wanted to piece together the reason Mark was leaving so that maybe this could be my chance to get out, too. *What does he know that I don't know?*

"Listen," he said. There was a tightness in his voice. Exhaustion? Frustration? Maybe something tinged with guilt because he knew that I'd trusted him when I entered this community and took the steps he recommended to stay in it, even when I felt unsure. "I want to fill you in, but the only way I can really tell you is if you'll sign a nondisclosure agreement." The moment he said this, I knew there was something at stake for him, too—he didn't trust the organization with his safety anymore.

Maybe someone else would have been insulted that a friend would request this, but I saw it as my only way to start finding more answers. Also, for us, nondisclosure agreements were typical company practice. NXIVM had always asked us upper levels and even its students to sign NDAs to protect their material. I'd heard Keith had tried time and again to patent some of his concepts and philosophies, but he hadn't been successful. The curriculum documents had always been marked with "patent pending" or a trademark, but later I would find out that many of Keith's applications for patents had apparently been denied, partly, I was told, because the U.S. Patent and Trademark Office deemed that his material wasn't actually original.

I'd sign Mark's nondisclosure agreement willingly if that's what it took for trust to be renewed between friends. It was obvious that he was trying to protect himself. We both knew that the upper levels were litigiously ruthless toward anyone who dared cross them.

I told him to send over the NDA, immediately signing it and scanning it back to him. Then I called him in L.A., relieved there was no bullshit between us when he cut right to the point. "What do you notice about the people who live in Albany?" he asked me. Inductive reasoning: a NXIVM technique. From the beginning we'd been trained to induce people's responses instead of giving them the answers. The NDA, Rational Inquiry—we'd used the tools to get in, and now we would use the tools to get out. I sat quietly, listening, while Mark continued. "Have you ever seen Keith do the things he says he does?"

"What do you mean?"

"Have you ever seen him write a module? Have you seen any of his credentials, like that IQ test that put him in the Guinness Book of World Records? He's supposed to be a trained classical pianist—have you ever seen him play? Or show off his Judo champion skills?" For all the times we'd been in settings when he'd arrested our attention, not once had I witnessed any of these supposed talents in person. "How do we know he is who he says he is?" Mark said. Then he dropped the bomb. "I've heard rumors—something about this new group of women supposedly gaining enlightenment through sex with Keith."

My heart fell through my stomach and crashed to the floor. In this single moment, twelve years culminated into one moment of pure clarity.

He went on, telling me that there was chatter in the community that in this new group being formed, a club of sorts, one young woman had been given an assignment to seduce Keith. She was instructed take a photo to prove that she'd done it, or risk having her collateral published. She'd been told, "You have permission to enjoy it." They actually thought we women would want to do this. *That asshole!* I thought. How dare they make these women do things they didn't want to and use their collateral against them!

Part of the problem was, with the big enrollment push, they were inviting women who had never taken Jness, who were not sufficiently indoctrinated to be all-in. Another part of their problem was that there was so much about this secret society that they hadn't thought through. In the two months since I'd received my brand, I'd managed to turn my body away or keep it covered to conceal it from my husband . . . but did they really think he'd never discover it and guess that it was tied to ESP? Now I had to ask myself: was this Keith's way of trying to break us up? Or were they actually that stupid? Was it a fuck-you to Nippy— Keith's way of telling him: *Sarah is mine—I own her now?*

While Mark continued speaking, everything stilled around me. I tried to take all this in. I'd been brought into DOS as Lauren's slave, not to join a sisterhood of empowered women. I'd been recruited so that I'd be one of the women forced to have sex with Keith—or more likely, given my age and weight above 110 pounds, they brought me in because I was so good at sales. I was the perfect leader to recruit pretty young women for Keith to have at his disposal. All of the women Lauren had urged me to bring in were extremely attractive. From the Vancouver center's Facebook page, she'd screenshot photos of women she didn't even know to suggest that I recruit them into DOS. The way they'd filmed the branding ceremony; the way they'd said we didn't look happy enough in the nude photos: now I was sure that every bit of it, along with our collateral, had been sent to Keith. I saw it so clearly now. It was like a blackmail pyramid scheme, and Keith was at the top.

I was conscious of the fact that somehow I wasn't totally shocked. *Right,* I thought. *Keith's a sociopath who for years has been training women to worship him so that they'll all have sex with him. Of course. This makes everything click into place.* It was like watching *The Sixth Sense.* Once you finally gain a certain piece of information at the end, so much lines up about everything that happened before. *Bruce Willis is dead!* And Keith Raniere is a sociopath. It was the same kind of epiphany, as I pieced it all together.

When I figured out that Keith wasn't who he said he was, I realized that could be attributed to one plain fact: Keith isn't smart in the way he claims to be. This program wasn't designed to be successful. Making this discovery was a relief in a way, because for the first time, all these things that had never lined up suddenly did. It now made sense that our administrative team was a constant clusterfuck and that nothing ever went smoothly. Or that, years ago, Keith had thwarted a meeting I'd set up with Nancy and Lululemon as we were hoping to sell our personal development curriculum to their staff. Or that Keith was always reluctant to upgrade the website or maybe rebrand our image from the 1990s kitsch and cheap sashes. At one point, in the early years when Mark and I were trying to get him to redo the 1998 ancient website, I heard him say that we didn't even need a website— that the company's success was all word of mouth. *In what century are you living?* I wondered. More like, *on what* planet *are you living?* To judge all of this normal and OK, Keith Raniere had to be living in another world.

But this understanding about NXIVM was followed immediately by a new concern about myself. *Oh my God, I'm in a cult. The media, my stepmother . . . over the years, people had said we were a cult, and they were right. I was wrong.* I flashed back to a memory when my agent teased me, saying I was going to Albany to shave my head and drink goats' blood. I remembered a time when one of my closest friends asked me to sit down with her husband, Pepe, who had "done his research online" and was not happy about what he'd found regarding NXIVM.

"I'm happy to answer any questions he has," I told her. Inside a café, Pepe sat me down and showed me *all* of the negative press about NXIVM while pressing me to explain it. Smoothly, I rolled into my answer about the smear campaign; how Keith had done such good in the world and how society pushes back at progress. Recently one of our students in New York City had started going to ESP classes. He was struggling with extreme Tourette syndrome, displaying tics and yelling profanities during the intensives. A side effect of his work on the Stripe Path was that his tics and outbursts had begun to subside. Nancy and Keith tried to duplicate this on a sample of Tourette's patients with stunning results. They seemed to have developed a cure for Tourette syndrome and even made a beautiful film documenting the process with five candidates who appeared to have the same rapid results. This type of proof was what kept me in toward the end of my time in NXIVM. I opened my laptop to show Pepe the Tourette's trailer and he shut my computer. "I believe you that there is good here. But I'm asking you about the *bad*."

This tough conversation with Pepe would plant a seed of doubt in me. He called me to consider that all these reports over the years must contain a grain of truth. Did Keith really lose millions of the Bronfmans' money in the stock market? Who were these underage girls he was accused of having relationships with? What about the lawsuits? For the first time I realized I really didn't know the answers.

We'd been taught not to question, when there'd been so much to question. The discovery that Mark and I were making validated that I wasn't crazy . . . but with every piece of knowledge about NXIVM came new questions about myself. *Am I stupid? Did I honestly fall for this? What was my motivation for staying in this for so long?*

Up to now, I'd been afraid of my DOS collateral being released, but as Mark and I spoke, I knew this was bullshit. Our nondisclosure agreement protected only Mark, but I felt strangely safe under it. For the first time in a long time we were two friends speaking freely. "The women's group?" I asked him. "Mark, I'm part of it. Lauren got me in, and it's worse than you think. They're branding us."

"They're *what?*" Mark was livid. He'd brought me into this organization, and I'd brought so many others. He felt responsible. I did, too. "You have to get out—fuck the collateral. *Fuck them!* This is all very dangerous, Sarah. I think this is sex trafficking."

By now my mind was spinning. It was as though the floor beneath me had caved in and the world around me shifted. It was the glitch in the matrix. I thought my head would explode.

We spent four hours on the phone dissecting the details and putting the pieces back together in a way that we could both see clearly. Mark revealed to me that for years, each time he'd encouraged me to commit myself deeper, to invest further, to foster a relationship with Keith, he'd done it because that's what the senior-level leaders were instructing him to do. It was like a virus. I hadn't fully understood that because Keith had been so good at keeping us siloed in separate cells from one another. He and the inner circle had taken what we believed was noble in the world and made us two of their key spokespeople, bringing thousands of other people in so Keith could choose the ones he wanted to use. They appealed to our morality, a tactic that I would later learn was characteristic of a cult.

Meanwhile, for so long, I'd thought, *Wow, here's a system that's actually talking about things in the world that need to be addressed instead of just giving lip service.* Not only was it lip service, it was destroying people's lives—and bodies.

As soon as I got off the phone with Mark I frantically called Susanna and asked her to come over right away. I needed an ally on the ground. "But I am coaching the intensive!" she protested. "Just tell them you are having a family emergency and just get here." Up until now, all of the puzzle pieces were floating around in my head as I tried to comprehend what I was a part of, but the breaking point came when I asked Susanna to take a look at the brand on my pelvis. "First of all," I told her, "you are not getting one of these." Together we stepped into the light . . . and it was here, as she studied the mark closely, that she discovered it wasn't a symbol that resembled nature or the elements. "You see that?" I asked her. "It's an *A* and an *M*. Do you think it stands for Allison Mack?"

Susanna looked straight on, tracing those two letters. But then, as she turned her head at a hard right angle, I saw her expression change. Susanna looked up at me. "Sarah," she said. "There's a K and an R."

Keith Raniere.

Oh.

My.

God.

Susanna held my arm as I had to brace myself and sit down. *No. No. No.* I looked at Susanna—my friend, *not* my slave—and her eyes held such sorrow for me. As I gazed at her sweet face, I was aware of the stark difference between the two of us. I had this marking. She didn't. Susanna's body remained unharmed only because of the sheer luck of timing. And it would stay that way, if I had anything to do with it.

Susanna took a seat next to me. The memories of the dozens, the hundreds of things I'd said yes to over the years came rushing through my brain. Nothing had been what I thought it was.

At this point there was no talking me out of my knowing that DOS was run by Keith. For years, they'd been grooming us for this, teaching us how women should respect and obey men. They'd preached that our leader was the most ethical humanitarian in the world, but in this instant, I saw Keith Raniere clearly for who he was. It had taken me twelve years to finally reach my own opinion, in the form of a permanent mark on my body.

Once we saw Keith's initials, I called Mark immediately, and now we had almost the whole picture. Nippy had been frustrated because Mark had recently withdrawn from a brand-new SOP III course that they were supposed to teach together. My husband wasn't even in town for me to share all this with him. He'd flown out east for a college reunion, and in a way, I thought it would go smoother if he heard it from Mark. Somehow this seemed safer—like I wasn't breaking my secrecy vow. I asked my friend: "Can you be the one to tell Nippy? *Please?*"

Again, under a separate NDA, the two of them set a time to have a phone call. That's when Mark revealed to my husband that I'd been branded. Mark was in L.A. Nippy was in New York. I was back in Vancouver. I wished that we were all in the same city; it was so hard to be physically alone as we uncovered all this.

But there was also so much relief in knowing that now it wouldn't just be me taking long walks and trying to figure out my options. The two people I trusted most were going to support me. Our three-way calls lasted hours as we tried to figure out what to do as we'd all begin to take back our lives.

Together, the three of us decided to stick with business as usual. We had the mandatory annual coach summit coming up the following week in Albany, and Nippy, Mark, and I agreed that my not going would draw too much attention. *I can't wait to see You!* I texted Lauren. We planned a sleepover for that week.

On May 29, I flew to New York City to celebrate Nippy's birthday. I hadn't seen him in person since we'd decided to leave, and I was shaking from nerves and lack of sleep when he greeted me at his parents' door in Manhattan. Sleepless nights and the flight with a toddler had left me barely functional. My husband held me and rubbed my back as I rested against the strong warmth of his body and took in his scent. I'd been so afraid that he wouldn't get it—but now, four months after Lauren had gotten me to take the vow of obedience and commit to DOS, here my husband and I stood, on the same page.

Making sure that our son was occupied in another room, I privately showed Nippy the brand. He stayed calm but began to pace the room, debating how he was going to handle this—another man's initials on his wife. But one thing was certain: we were both done. I explained how Lauren had deceived me, and never once did he say: "How could you let them brand you?!" He knew them, and he got it.

The next day, on May 30, I was supposed to be at a green meeting in Albany before the summit. I texted the team that I'd gotten stuck in highway traffic on my way to the meeting, but the truth was that Mark had contacted a friend, a DEA agent we could trust who had a connection to the FBI. Mark had set up the meeting for me and an agent there. I was about to walk in and show him my brand to explain the intricacies of DOS.

The anticipation leading up to this meeting with the FBI was one of the most terrifying times of my life. I felt there was a chance that I'd be in trouble. I'd recruited a couple of women into DOS, and essentially, I was coming in and saying, "I'm part of this thing." I'd been involved in it, though not knowing what it was. Still, I worried that I was surrendering. They took away my electronic devices and asked me to sit for an hour. Maybe less, but it felt like forever. Without my phone, I was forced to sit with my feelings. No—instead I rummaged through my purse and proceeded to apply every product I could find: lip balm, hand sanitizer, eye drops, nose spray, hand cream, aromatherapy for stress. *How had I ended up there? Should I have had a lawyer? Would I be locked up? Would they believe me?*

I looked up just as another woman I knew from ESP walked out into the waiting area with the FBI agent. Mark had let me know I might see a familiar face. *Oh my God,* I thought. *She looks so good.* She was a lower ranking coach who'd been in the community for as long as I could remember. After Pam died, this woman had also been diagnosed with a terminal illness.

For several reasons, I was so relieved to see her. She had a fighting chance at life—and, we both knew what was going on. *I have an ally in this,* I thought. *I'm not alone anymore.* I hadn't seen her in months; a year maybe. She looked better, maybe because she was no longer following Keith's protocol. With her there, I didn't have to hold the toxic pain of this secret anymore. I could let go and risk everything to help my friends. To free the slaves.

Once they brought me in to speak with the agent, I was in that room for an hour, though I wasn't sure if he really understood my story. I tried so hard to show him, this poor investigator. But how do you pack twelve years into one hour?

When I left the FBI building, I returned to the condo we'd kept in Albany for the past three years. Our nanny looked after our child while I stayed up all night to pack everything that was valuable to me from our place. We would need to make a fast exit.

I had a legitimate reason to leave Albany: my grandfather in Toronto had been diagnosed with stomach cancer, and I was going to say goodbye to him. It would be a ten-hour train ride, but I told the senior levels that I'd try to make it back to Albany for the summit. Instead, while my son was protected with headphones and an iPad, I called everyone I knew and told them not to go to the summit. Paige was back in Vancouver and was just about to board her flight, and I was afraid she'd be more loyal to NXIVM than she would be to me. I had to warn her and scare her enough that she would know how serious this was. "I know you're supposed to go see Nicki and get your tattoo," I said. "But it's not a tattoo. I need you to Facetime me." On camera, I peeled back the top of my pants and showed her.

"What *is* that?" she said.

"It's a brand that you're supposed to get without anesthetic, and it's not a pretty design. It's Keith's initials and Allison's initials. You are not getting on that plane." Paige went into shock, convulsing as I told her the truth. Immediately she cancelled her flight. Nicki was not happy: I had stopped the branding of Paige and her sisters.

On the train from Albany to Toronto, while my son slept with his head against my arm, I wrote about my experience. Ten hours from Albany to Toronto with a three-year-old, an iPad, and a bag full of food. How had I ended up here? *So alone and scared*, I wrote, *and yet strong and certain.*

Those long moments of sitting, waiting for the train to take us away. My stomach full of anxious knots: What if they find out? As I boarded the train in Albany, a dear friend, Jack, was getting off the same train, having traveled from New York. I knew I'd never see him again. I held him so tight, so desperately wanting to scream the truth so he would run too. But I knew he wouldn't believe me. He would warn the others. He would reveal me, with good intentions, and my cover would have been blown. Instead, I just cried and told him about my grandpa's worsening condition. He hugged me back, sincerely concerned.

I spent the entire train ride so much in action mode that by the time I reached Toronto, I was fried. I'd made plans to stay with a friend there, but with my son and all our luggage in tow, I could not locate an Uber. Frazzled, in tears, and at the end of my rope, I called Nippy. "Babe," he said. "I know that area. Look right across the street from where you're standing." I glanced across, spotting the Shangri-La Hotel. "Go there. I'll pay for it. This is our exit cost."

Hand in hand, my son and I raced across the street and entered the hotel as the staff at the reception desk worked graciously to get us a room.

Once we were settled and I had set my child up to watch a movie, the first thing I did was call my lawyer in Vancouver to have her amend my will. I had named Lauren as the legal guardian for my son, and I had to change that immediately. While I was on the phone with her, I saw a text come through from my acting agent, who was writing to ask if I would be free the following week to appear in a supporting role in a TV movie he'd asked me to audition for. "But I missed that audition," I told him. He responded, saying the casting director didn't care; that they were offering me the role anyway. I accepted. At the exact time, I saw an email come through from my voice agent, informing me that a national advertising campaign that I had worked on for a major U.S. brand was coming through with new spots, and that she had more work for me. Right then I knew that the universe was supporting me in my exit from NXIVM. All these career opportunities would provide a financial buffer so that finances wouldn't be a stress through this as I walked away from the past twelve years of my life and everything I had built.

In our hotel room, safe like a sanctuary, I thought back to the train ride and my escape: *they fucked with the wrong woman.* Later, when DOS was exposed and the slaves from the different pods started to communicate and share their harrowing stories, one of the other slaves called me "the original abolitionist." It could have sounded offensive, out of context, to anyone other than me, but this paled in comparison to the absurdity of DOS—women choosing to become enslaved in order to "empower and grow" themselves. I embraced the nickname, as I embraced the woman who'd used it along with my other sisters, whom I'd helped to free. That train ride was the beginning of my journey to freedom, truth, and the next chapter of my life.

CHAPTER FOURTEEN

BREACH FORM

2017

I had a huge decision to make: slip away quietly, or blow this thing up. The answer became clear to me within a few days as I started to realize how big DOS had become. I wanted to protect other women, but I had to be careful to avoid a defamation lawsuit. We talked to cult experts, therapists, and a few people we knew in the media to figure out how to manage it. We had to develop a plan to outwit the schemers.

When I arrived in Toronto, I called my assistant and asked her to clean everything about NXIVM off my LinkedIn page and all my social media, my website, everywhere. At that point, Mark had told the actress Catherine Oxenberg about the branding and the intricacies of DOS. We'd deduced that Catherine's daughter, India, was in DOS as a slave under Allison Mack. Catherine was in mama bear mode to get her out.

Catherine begged me to tell my story to a reporter named Frank Parlato, who'd been in a long legal fight with the Bronfman sisters. He had once been hired by the Bronfmans to do some PR, but the Bronfmans ended up suing him. Since then, he'd made it his life's work to uncover information about the workings of NXIVM and blog about it. Under the condition that he would not disclose my name, I told Frank about my branding experience, so that he could expose DOS in time to stop the next session. From my hotel room in Toronto, I told Frank everything. Releasing that secret was the biggest relief so far.

We were successful. The word about Frank's blog spread in the community, and because of this heat the next branding ceremony was called off. From this point on, every move we'd make had to be highly strategic, and we would all need to be in step with each other.

Meanwhile, as my son and I had journeyed from Albany to Toronto, Nippy arrived in Albany for the NXIVM coaches' summit. When my husband reached the parking lot of Apropos, the restaurant-turned-NXIVM clubhouse where the summit was being held, he tracked down Lauren Salzman, who was talking with one of Nippy's longtime SOP mentors, Jim. My husband surveyed the scene to make sure there was a crowd nearby—and then he yelled: "*YOU BRANDED MY FUCKING WIFE!*" Lauren tried to calm him down and use her ESP rapport skills to enter a conversation, but Nippy wasn't having any of it. He warned Lauren she was participating in illegal activities and announced his resignation from all the companies. This was Nippy's "mic drop." He was the only person ever to publicly confront Lauren or anyone in the upper ranks about DOS.

As some of the people nearby heard his accusation and looked on in concern, Nippy walked away and got into his car, knowing he'd accomplished his part of our plan. We were both leaving NXIVM. We wanted all of them to know that it was because of what they'd done to me, and that Nippy was not OK with it. If they thought my loyalty to the community was more powerful than my trust in my husband to stand up for me . . . then, as Mark said: fuck them.

For years, the senior-level leaders had focused on what they called my issues of dependency in order not to promote me to a green sash. Now we'd use this "attachment to my relationship" as my excuse to safely get out. Nippy had gotten angry and made a scene, which was also consistent with the way they viewed his personality. *See?* they'd think. *Nippy's having a reaction and Sarah's buying in. She's so weak.* But this was what he and I both wanted. Together we were getting out.

Our logic for using this strategy was that it would be the only real way to make a clean break. This was the best advice we had been given by someone who had left a few months earlier: you can't just leave a cult, especially NXIVM. Anyone who directly confronted Keith, like Barbara Bouchey, ended up getting dragged through the legal system for years. Keith had been effective at using Barbara as a scapegoat and example for others. But if you left because of your "issues," it would be easy for the upper ranks to say, "Sarah never worked through her issues . . . so sad." People who'd departed quietly were left alone, but they were *always* painted as having failed at their personal evolution.

Ironically this was probably the first time that my character was actually tested. I was traumatized, but I was thinking very clearly. *I need to do this carefully.* I recorded myself on a call with Lauren Salzman from Toronto right after Nippy's calculated tantrum. I wanted to see if she would continue to lie to me. I told her that Nippy wanted a divorce (he did not), and that this was the reason I had to leave. "Was Keith behind DOS?" I asked her pointedly, already knowing the answer.

"It's not something that we discussed, Sarah," she said, clearly exasperated with me.

"But Keith gave his go-ahead on it?"

For a second, she hesitated. "He gave them permission to use collateral and penance."

"OK, so he didn't know about the branding?"

"He knew about it, but he didn't *cause* it. The girls did." She was trying to tell me Keith wasn't responsible, which I knew was bullshit.

"This is not what I signed up for, Lauren. I'm sorry. I don't want to do this anymore."

"We wanted to do something good for the world!" she went on. "It wasn't supposed to be a horrible experience."

"I need to step back from you."

When I asked her about women getting assignments to "seduce Keith" or to have sex with him, she denied it.

"I was not part of that!" she tried to tell me. "I just got involved recently!"

But she did know about it. And in her role pushing for new recruits, she *was* involved—and she'd been leading it. Our phone call also confirmed what I'd been strongly suspecting since my phone conversation with Mark: that Keith knew about DOS and had been in on it. I was disgusted by Lauren's complicity and willingness to lie.

It was time to sever ties officially. I wrote a formal letter of resignation and submitted it to the executive board in Albany so that a record of my departure would exist in writing.

At this point, quietly slipping back into my life was not an option. I was determined to fix what I'd started. I told Lauren that she could take over the Vancouver center, but meanwhile Nippy and I were warning the people in our community to get out, and word spread quickly. Immediately I told the three women I had called my slaves that the whole thing was off and that I would explain more in person. I hated myself for having led them astray. I knew they would be angry with me, as I was with Lauren, but hoped that they would understand that I never lied to them. It was Lauren who had lied to me, and I had done her bidding to please her, to be mentored by her, and to keep growing up the Stripe Path. I felt so ashamed for having dismissed the red flags in favor of the promise of a sisterhood.

I felt responsible. I knew that I hadn't done the bad thing to them, but I'd set them up to experience it. I owned that, and now I had to stop it from going any further.

I continued to reach out to every woman I could think of who might have been invited into DOS. As word spread about what was happening—and it did, fast—enrollment at our Vancouver center instantly tanked. I went onto the Vancouver ESP community page on Facebook, which was how we all communicated. Since I was the administrator, I kicked off Nicki, Allison, and Clare, and everyone who was still loyal to the various companies under NXIVM. My former assistant, Angie, had already used her old login and canceled all of our members' future payments. A solo, brave act that Clare would later use to try to get Angie arrested for fraud.

After Nippy confronted Lauren at the summit, people were quitting by the time we both made it back to Vancouver in early June. Almost everybody in Vancouver was out. Most didn't know about the branding or what the disagreement was, but they felt: *If Nippy and Sarah are out, then we've lost trust in NXIVM too.*

But it wasn't over—not even close. I knew there would be consequences. They'd take me to court, they'd wipe out my finances, and they would say terrible things and slander my character in the community that had been my closest friends for over a decade. I remembered their smear campaign against Barbara Bouchey and the NXIVM Nine, so I had to be careful. I continued moving faster than they were.

I didn't speak about my brand. Everyone was reading Frank's blog, so in combination with Nippy's words to Lauren in the Apropos parking lot, other Espians had started to put together what had happened. I was redirecting phone calls to Ariella, one of the proctors in Vancouver, who was a dear friend. She'd never been a chief enroller in NXIVM, but now—disgusted about the branding—she was very good at de-enrolling people from the community. She didn't have any collateral on the line and was happy to tell them everything that was going on. Ariella became my mouthpiece.

She texted me: *Can you please talk to Beth? She is supposed to move to Albany and doesn't believe the Frank Report.* She was referring to Frank Parlato's blog.

Sure, I texted back. I was just dropping my child at daycare but wanted to make sure that Beth, an introverted and highly intelligent young scientist, didn't move to Albany anytime soon. "I am at work," she said when I called her. "Let me step out, and I'll call you right back."

When she did, she had many questions and I tried to direct her to the *Frank Report.* "But it can't be true, right?" she said. "I mean—*branding?* I'm supposed to move to Albany and this shit is scary."

Her question sent me over the edge. "For fuck's sake, Beth—do you need to see my brand?"

She was silent on the line.

"Do *not* move to Albany. Trust me." I hung up the phone, shaking, thinking I had saved another woman from the trap I had just escaped from.

Instead, I found out a few hours later from Melanie, another DOS slave who came to me for help after she read Frank's blog, that not only was Beth *in* DOS, but she was Melanie's master, and had already been branded. Beth had been tasked with recording me breaking my vow of secrecy. That was why she said she had to step out of work to call me back—to set up the "tape a call" app that I'd used with Lauren the week before. That why she had so many questions: she was setting me up. That's also why almost everyone cut contact with me after that phone call with Beth. Her master was one of the first-line DOS slaves directly under Keith, on the same level as Lauren. Now Keith would know I was a defector. He'd also know I was not going away quietly. My cover was blown.

As the red alert on my status in NXIVM spread around the remaining community, I prepared to come forward. I knew what they would call me: suppressive, destructive, a weak woman having a tantrum. But I had to keep warning people. Hearing that Melanie had been recruited brought me to a new level of anger. She was a lower level coach in Vancouver, and she shared with me that she had given an extremely personal photo for collateral, per her master's orders. I had no doubt this photo had gone to Keith, and I was furious. Melanie was part of my team and I was very protective. Being taped only fueled me to keep warning people like my friend Oscar, who had left a six-figure job in New York City to join NXIVM in Albany. When he sent me a message to ask if we could talk, I showed him a photo of my brand and he started to cry. Two days later, he left Albany.

The responses from people I knew, and had even enrolled, weren't always as validating. Ross, my friend and right hand at the Vancouver center, was upset I was leaving. But after he spoke with Lauren about it, I received a text from him that read, *I'm not buying the bullshit fantasy victim drama you're selling.* I was so pissed, I texted Lauren, *It's time for you to fill out a Breach form.*

Speaking of ethical breaches, I was learning that Keith was the ultimate parasite or grifter. He never paid bills, never provided for these women, never even cooked for himself. They had all done everything for him, right down to driving. And now, equipped with this truth about him, I was ready to fight back.

Unfortunately, we had received little support from law enforcement initially, so the next attempt for exposure would be the media. Friends gave us contacts, including Barry Meier, then a reporter for the *New York Times*. If we were going to blow this up and let the world know, we had to go with one of the most credible outlets. We decided to speak with him.

In mid-June, I told Barry off the record what had happened. Eventually, Mark; his wife, Bonnie; Catherine Oxenberg; Nippy; and I all agreed to go on the record.

It took weeks to get everybody to agree at the same time, but ultimately we knew that if we were going to put a permanent stop to what was happening to these women, we had to stick together. Because Bonnie had left months before us, she had started to collect resources about cults: how to know if you are in one, how to leave one, and links to various shows and documentaries that would help us to deprogram. Watching people like Leah Remini and documentaries about other alleged cults like *Holy Hell* and *Going Clear* inspired me to go public beyond the *Frank Report*. We decided we wouldn't go down without a fight.

Cult experts advised us that the more chaos we could create— the more fires we could start—the harder it would be for Keith and his inner circle to defend against our accusations. To ensure our own safety, we had to throw the biggest punch possible.

Weeks went by. I received a cease and desist letter from lawyers in Mexico, advising me to "stop, abstain, and refrain from incurring in any type of intimidation, acts of nuisance, or disturbances." Barry Meier interviewed two other women from inside DOS, who agreed to speak only on condition of anonymity, and researchers at the *Times* fact-checked the story. One of the women backed out and said she didn't want her story told, and then she came around just as the other woman backed out in fear. There were so many moving parts, and we needed every single one of them to work together. For just a little longer.

We waited and waited . . . and waited. July turned to August and August to September. As we waited, what would have been my thirteenth V-Week was held. We even called the Silver Bay resort and told them what was happening, but we knew they'd lose significant business if V-Week wasn't held. The event remained scheduled.

This was the scariest time. *What are they waiting for?* we wondered. What if Keith somehow found out we'd been talking to the press and was lining up his response? Or, even more worrisome, what if the *Times* didn't find our report all that relevant and the story got squashed? Barry tried to assure us that his editors were waiting for a break in the news cycle, which was filled with coverage of Trump's first year in office. We knew there was nothing we could do to persuade them to move faster.

Then, in October 2017, Harvey Weinstein's predatory behavior was exposed, igniting the #MeToo movement. The editors at the *Times* finally saw this as their window to publish our story, and on Wednesday, October 18, it ran on the front page of the *New York Times*, accompanied by my image with the headline: "Branding Ritual Scarred Women in Secret Circle." As my eyes raced through the article, I realized they'd shortened it. They'd omitted the account from the anonymous woman from DOS. *See?* I knew Keith and the upper ranks would explain it away. *Sarah's the only one having a tantrum.* This wouldn't impact the NXIVM community; I knew they could use this to sell The Knife Media curriculum to "educate" students on the way Keith believes the media works to slant data. I held on to my courage. It was the women who were coming forward as part of #MeToo who demonstrated to me that true power is to use your voice.

I was terrified, but I was on a mission to protect and save everyone I could. I learned from cult expert Janja Lalich that this reaction, referred to as the "savior complex," was normal for someone leaving a cult. My next step was to shut down my center before anyone from Albany could intervene. I sent out a group text to fifteen Espians, who all met me at the center. We divided into teams to pack, clean, and move out. Some of them held up a large posterboard we'd had on the wall that featured the faces of some of the company's executives (including me), while I and a couple others karate-chopped it and tore it apart, screaming: "*Fuck you, Vanguard!*" The tears and primal screams were not only cathartic, but they were the first time in years that we were no longer suppressing how we really felt. Then, to feed everyone who had kindly shown up to help, I called and ordered pizza . . . with meat.

I'd thought of recording the closing of the center, but I didn't because I was still afraid of Clare and her weaponized legal strategies.

It turned out I was right, and I was about to face the scariest moment of all.

In July 2017, Angie told me she saw Clare Bronfman walking on the seawall in Stanley Park, which borders downtown Vancouver. A month later, in August, the police phoned me and said Clare had accused me of criminal fraud, mischief, and theft. I'd already handed over notes, iPads, old sashes, and all the training materials to the other Vancouver coaches who remained loyal to NXIVM, but I had refused to hand over twelve boxes of student files, with our members' personal records and financial details. I did not trust the senior ranks to safeguard all of that sensitive information that could be used to further blackmail the community I had built. Those people and their safety were precious to me.

It was Pepe, who'd recently sat me down and forced me to read old NXIVM headlines, who would offer his assistance in obtaining the best criminal defense lawyer in Vancouver. He helped me navigate the Vancouver Police Department and assured me I did nothing wrong in withholding the client files. Clare also told the police that my IP address was linked to financial crimes that had been committed, but investigators found that I wasn't even where Clare said I'd been on specific dates. Eventually, after a lengthy investigation, the police would drop the charges against me. No fraud was committed, as I hadn't stolen money. Angie had merely stopped payments, and when the police contacted my student list, each one confirmed they no longer wanted to continue with ESP in Vancouver.

It was all so ludicrous that Clare was painting *me* to be the criminal. By this time the *New York Times* article had been published. It was clear to the authorities who was the whistleblower and who was the bully. Around this time, Barbara Bouchey contacted me. Nippy and I spent many hours on the phone with her, talking through the events of the past years and apologizing for shunning her. She put me in touch with Neil Glazer, a passionate lawyer with a penchant for justice and women's rights, who agreed to take me on as his client.

It seemed obvious to me that Keith was trying to cut off any potential threats, and I was sure that he had sent Clare to Vancouver to silence me. Nippy helped me think through the solution to every issue that came up, and we knew we had to get out in front of their legal playbook. Going public and exposing Keith Raniere and the entire DOS scheme was a huge part of that goal. But we also understood the repercussions: going public also meant opening ourselves up to criticism. Ultimately, my greater concern was to take care of my community—especially the women who had inadvertently given collateral to a sociopath.

CHAPTER FIFTEEN

FREEDOM

2017–2019
VANCOUVER

During the week of Thanksgiving 2017, I spent two and a half grueling days with the FBI as they formally planned their criminal investigation of NXIVM. The first thing Moira Penza, the Assistant United States Attorney I was working with, said to me was: "Thank you for going public. Your story is what initiated this investigation." Then she added: "Please don't talk anymore. Doing more press will discredit you as a good witness."

I obliged, slightly concerned about the few things I had already started: a piece for A&E about cults; a podcast called *Uncover: Escaping NXIVM* that a childhood friend was producing for the CBC, Canada's biggest news outlet; and a documentary that had captured so much of my experience leaving the group. The investigation was in the FBI's hands now. I had given them everything: multiple bankers boxes full of notes, everything on my computer and phone. I had nothing to hide. With Neil by my side, I knew that Moira and her team at the Department of Justice would help me. Still, I was dealing with the aftermath of leaving a cult. Sheer anger fueled my mission. Privately, I was still reeling. Nippy helped me articulate my experience for interviews and held me on days when I couldn't function. I used journal entries to help me process:

I am aching to purge. To find the wise woman within me and to perform a ritual of exorcism. To wrestle out the wiring, to twist out the hooks of the angry chords stretching so far from Albany to keep me unwittingly engaged. I've grown to hate these people; friends I once trusted with my life, my secrets, my dreams. They have become shadows, soulless and mean. Punishing, gossiping, lying trolls; empty shells of who they once were.

And I am out here stranded, violently trying to assemble my life back together. I am harvesting normalcy. Safety. Security. Warmth. Kindness. Connection. Owning them. Standing up and announcing proudly: This is what I want!

This is who I am.

I am harvesting my SELF. I am mending all the broken shards of my soul back into a whole person. And with every recovery I am gently reminded that never was I actually broken—I was never deficient. I was always whole and complete.

I am making the time, carving out space to extract the voice that I put aside for 12 years. I'm finding my creative outlet and time for me . . . finally. I am harvesting my JOY. Authentic joy. Not robotic, faux joy. I am harvesting my forgotten freedom and play so I can join my son on the floor with his Lego masterpieces and get lost in a castle with monsters and thunderstorms.

I will discover my self again. Flushed and wrung out. Hanging fresh and laundered, swaying off a clothesline in the backyard of a simple burnt red farmhouse; wild green grass against bluebird sky and sun purifying the whole scene . . . but especially me. I am clean again. I know that through this process I will have forgiven those who betrayed me; who threw me under the bus. Who gaslit me and scavenged my delicate naive mind to replace my beliefs with theirs. I will let go of the rage, just dance in the breeze with that clothesline . . . swaying, calm.

I will be me again one day: Mama. Wife. Actress. Yogi. Smoothie junkie.

I am grounded

rooted

peaceful.

I will feel grateful for my journey. I will have told my story and can move on. I will have lived the beginning, middle and end of those chapters of my life. My entire thirties. It's done now.

The pain will leave my body to form words and educational passageways for others to find their way out of their own darkness; a map for the friends I left behind and even for those I never met. Together we'll meld back as a whole community once again. Stronger, wiser. Invincible.

In March 2018—just shy of a year after Mark and I had realized what we'd been part of, and one year after I'd been branded with Keith Raniere's initials—Mexican authorities found Keith after a monthlong FBI search. He was hiding inside a villa in Mexico with a group of women that included Lauren Salzman, Allison Mack, and Nicki Clyne. News outlets in the U.S. reported that when the police pulled away with Keith in the back of their car, the women ran after them. Even though the police had seized him, they remained devoted.

Soon a photo circulated of Keith in the back of that police car. I'd never before seen him look haggard or scared. *Ah,* I thought. *So this is who Keith really is.* Call me suppressive, but it brought me such satisfaction to finally see him so exposed.

The leader formerly known as Vanguard was transported from Mexico to Texas and then eventually to Brooklyn via bus.

A few weeks later at the apartment she kept in Brooklyn, Allison Mack was arrested. She spent just a few nights in jail before she was released on bail of five million dollars and granted house arrest at her parents' home in Orange County, California.

My hope was that eating some proper meals and getting some sleep—away from Keith's daily manipulation—would help wake her up. After Allison's arrest, the dominoes fell with Lauren, Clare, Nancy, and Kathy Russell, the NXIVM bookkeeper, all getting arrested too. I wanted these women to pay for what they'd done to us . . . but I realized that even more than that, I wanted my former friends to heal.

Less than three months after his arrest, in June 2018, the FBI had gathered a great deal of evidence against Keith Raniere, including a series of text messages I read between Keith and one of my former friends, though the way the affidavit had been written, I couldn't tell who had participated in this dialogue with Keith because the FBI was keeping her anonymous. This text exchange occurred on October 9, 2015, just over a month after Barb J.'s death, and appeared in the June 2018 FBI court filing I read:

> RANIERE: I think it would be good for you to own a fuck toy slave for me, that you could groom, and use as a tool, to pleasure me . . .
>
> [DOS Slave]: huh?
>
> [DOS Slave]: not disagreeing, just don't understand
>
> RANIERE: But your [sic] my wife . . . she isn't . . . just a tool for you to use for me . . .
>
> [DOS Slave]: a person?
>
> RANIERE: Get a slave . . . you're her master . . .
>
> Without going into detail. It caused there to be other slaves, all who want to be branded with my monogram plus a number . . . your number is reserved . . . it is number 1. It is now a secret growing organization. I don't know well some of the people involved but I command them ultimately. They are not who you might think . . . I think there are ten or more in the current Jness track . . . and others outside of it.
>
> [DOS Slave]: Does that mean that they know about each other?
>
> RANIERE: No.
>
> [DOS Slave]: I'm ok with you having other slaves, I assume that these are not sexual
>
> RANIERE: They may or may not be. They would be if I commanded but that is not the reason for the organization. It is an absolutely trusted commitment . . .

[DOS Slave]: I want to be the one that worships your body

[DOS Slave]: Many will not even know of my existence . . . some don't already . . .

RANIERE: Find a life slave and I'll tell you everything . . .

[DOS Slave]: What do you mean by life slave?

RANIERE: Someone who has a collateralized vow with you for life . . .

RANIERE: I feel badly each time you have to work hard for me to [orgasm] . . . I thought slaves could remove the burden . . . and I could get you fresh and not worn

What are your thoughts feelings? All of them have slaves in process . . . some have several completed . . .

[DOS Slave]: I feel insecure but at the same time I feel proud of you. You are worthy of following like that

RANIERE: So are you . . . you're number one . . .

[DOS Slave]: I would be proud to stand next to you

RANIERE: Even naked with six other committed naked women?

[DOS Slave]: Ok. I'm asking because these persons will be in our life forever . . . But I was not involved in the process of choosing who

I'm afraid that I will not be comfortable with the others

RANIERE: You choose your slaves . . .

There are two types. Both types are for us. One type is in the program: you are their Master I am their Grand Master . . . the other type are very select ones you use to heal us: likely being also of the first type . . .

[DOS Slave]: What about the seven?

Allison said these seven were forever. She and the others will be forever in my life . . .

RANIERE: They are first line to me but if any suit the purpose I obviously have access . . .

[H]aving one or two young slaves devoted to revving my body sexual to produce more energy would help. It would be there [sic] 24/7 job . . .

So there it is. Keith not only knew about DOS, but he'd created DOS and was the Grandmaster above the eight first-line slave women below him. But today, as I write this, Keith sits in jail in Brooklyn as a convicted criminal awaiting sentencing.

■ ■ ■

In June 2017, I turned forty years old surrounded by my old friends, the same group who'd started *The Artist's Way* with me almost twenty years earlier. During my time in DOS, I had never bought that piece of jewelry that Lauren had instructed me to wear to represent my role as a slave . . . but on my birthday, one of these dear friends gifted me with a necklace. As I untied the ribbon and lifted the lid on the box, I discovered inside a key-shaped pendant. Attached to a gold chain, the key read *Love*.

My friends watched as I gathered my hair to one side to drape the chain around my collarbone and clasp it behind my neck. Emotional, I stood before them. For the first time since I'd joined NXIVM twelve years before, I'd chosen to love and stand up for myself, instead of blindly following Lauren or anyone else. And now, with these women I'd known for decades, I was surrounded by friends who truly cared for me.

But the saga was far from over. As I was finding my footing outside of NXIVM and reclaiming my former identity, Nippy and I woke up every morning to a message from a lawyer, a friend, or a former DOS slave who had an even darker story than we knew about what had been going on in Albany. FBI affidavits would eventually reveal one heinous detail after another: an account of a woman being led naked and blindfolded, then being held down while an unidentified person performed oral sex on her. Women were blackmailed into secrecy and branded. This type of intimidation, silencing, and blackmail would form the basis of the racketeering charges against NXIVM, along with forced labor and sex trafficking. NXIVM was a criminal enterprise.

Let's be clear: if Clare had been successful with the police department on her trip to Vancouver, I would be the one in prison right now.

Around this time Kristen Keeffe got in touch with me and shared how proud she was for my role in all of this. She revealed that she had escaped NXIVM with the help of the Albany police. Gaelen was actually Kristin's son. Not an orphan, but Keith's first child, and Kristin and Gaelen had been in hiding from Keith since she'd fled the community.

Kristin also gave me a key piece of advice. She suggested that I file a complaint with the New York State Department of Health. On June 22, 2017, that's exactly what I did—but when the department responded, they said there was nothing they could do as Danielle had not been my doctor at the time she branded me. Her case is still pending with the Department of Health.

After I spoke with Kristin and a series of other defectors who contacted me once they heard it was "out," I understood that Keith would go to any length to hide the truth, but I also learned the answer to one of the greatest mysteries of all: the "someone in the organization" whom Lauren had been involved with was Keith. He counted her as one of his spiritual wives, as they'd been in a relationship off and on for almost twenty years. Once a year, Lauren would ask Keith whether he would finally father her child. And each year, he would promise her a baby after she'd "worked through more of her shit"—meaning her life issue, or her Inner Deficiency. He called her "Forlorn," a pun on the name Lauren, to point out her suffering. I would find out that he had been manipulating her by promising her a child. I hated Keith for this and, knowing how much Lauren wanted to be a mom and the joy that motherhood had brought to my own life, I felt a deep sadness for my friend and everything she'd endured.

I also learned the truth about Barbara Bouchey. She was also not only a senior field trainer and financial expert, but one of the many women Keith counted as his partners, though she *thought* she was his exclusive girlfriend. The accusations she'd made as part of the NXIVM Nine had to do with the fact that she'd loaned him a million dollars, which he'd lost in the commodities market.

Every single one of these women had loved Keith. In turn, he'd destroyed them. As I started to share what I'd learned with some of my friends who had been in the program, one told me that Keith had proposed a romantic relationship to her and told her that he was cleansing his harem of older, longtime lovers to make room for fresh "nubile" young blood. "There will be a changing of the guard," he'd said. Another friend revealed to me that while she was doing an intensive on the Bronfmans' island in Fiji, Keith had asked her whether she wanted his one-on-one help in working on her issues. The first step, he said, would be to break up with her boyfriend because staying in that relationship meant that she would be putting her energy into that deficiency cover-up. "I'll need your full attention to work the issues," he told her. She turned him down.

I hope Keith is working his own issues with as much attention. While Keith was awaiting his federal trial, it was postponed three times because of the amount of evidence that the FBI had to investigate. The agents on Keith's case stated that they had the equivalent of about 144 library floors of data from searches to the defendants' homes. Twelve terabytes of evidence were found in Nancy's home alone, equivalent to approximately twenty-four million photos, or twenty-four full-length movies.

In spring 2019, Nancy Salzman was the first of Keith's women to plead guilty. Like Allison Mack, Nancy and Lauren had not been forced to sit in jail—in part because Nancy, like at least two of Keith's other closest executives, was facing a serious illness.

Lauren was the next to plead, followed immediately by Allison Mack. Then, after a dramatic fainting spell in court, Clare Bronfman pled guilty in April 2019. Kathy pleaded guilty the same day. Lauren's plea and Allison's were particularly poignant to me. Lauren, forty-two years old at the time, stated in court before a federal judge in Brooklyn that she had knowingly and intentionally helped imprison a young woman inside a room for almost two years and threatened to deport her back to Mexico if she did not complete labor requested by herself and Keith.

"I'm very sorry for my poor decision-making," Lauren stated, "and decisions that result in the harm to others and not just the victims in this case but to hundreds of members of our community and their friends and families as well." Weeks later, in May 2019, Lauren took the stand as a witness in Keith Raniere's federal trial. There, she and others—including a sales representative from a company in California that sold and shipped sex toys to one of Keith's first-line slaves—revealed more details that I'd never known: they had in fact ordered a human-size cage that cost $1,500 to punish women if someone hadn't followed Keith's commands. From the trial transcripts, Lauren confirmed that one of the first line DOS slaves had purchased a home for the "sorority" for the sole purpose of putting a sex dungeon in the basement.

The trial provided closure to many unanswered gaps from my time in NXIVM. First, that Pam and Barb J. were not the mentors I had thought them to be. Both were liars, having propped up the myth of Keith Raniere as a celibate genius while acting as his pimps, bringing women in for the sole purpose of having sex with him, even taking women for abortions when necessary. I also found out that the initials were only for Keith, not for Allison—but it didn't matter at that point as the transcripts revealed that she was complicit in worse ways as a leader in DOS.

As for Lauren, she had been in love with Keith, but he had chosen to father a second child with one of the women in Mexico while requiring Lauren to run errands for him and the mother of his child. There was a risk that if Lauren didn't cater to them, her collateral would be released. There were so many details about the sexually deviant acts Keith had called these women to perform for him . . . and he'd developed a very specific strategy for how he was going to finally have sex with me. After I'd joined DOS, Keith asked Lauren whether I was committed. She'd told him yes, that I was. Keith told Lauren that now I had to make her my priority over everything, including my family . . . and that if she asked me to have sex with someone other than Nippy,

I would have to obey and even have another man's child. Lauren said, under oath, that Keith seemed really excited about this.

■ ■ ■

Just days before my attorney gave me the heads-up that the news about all the guilty pleas was about to break, I'd had a lunch date at our favorite healthy restaurant with both my mom and dad. "The day you came to us and told us you were going to the *New York Times*," my dad said, "you were like a prizefighter getting ready to go into the ring." At our table toward the back of the restaurant, he reached for my hand, suddenly breaking down and weeping. "I'm so proud of you," he said.

"I feel like I've got my daughter back," my mom said, taking my other hand. "Remember how close we always were?"

"How come you never tried to pull me out of it?" I asked her.

"Because it was your life," she said. "And I didn't want to lose you. My connection with you was always the most important thing. And we never knew the full extent." She and my dad had obliged my request for them to take a NXIVM course called Family Values, focused on how extended family can work together for the well-being of the child. "The truth is," my mom said at lunch, "I was worried about your family." Even when I'd refused to read the headlines about events like Gaelen in the Rainbow experiment, my mother, out of her concern for our well-being, had done her research.

The ones who truly love you will always love you, and that's by far been the greatest lesson in all of this. Turns out my highest value is family after all. Having my child hold me when I pick him up, his arms around me, is pure bliss—more than I could ask for to have such a loving child.

What's brought this whole experience around for me most meaningfully is that in a way, maybe I've done what I set out to do. I got into NXIVM because I wanted to help others, to evolve the world and live and work among an empowered community of women. If Mark Vicente had asked me on that cruise, "Would you like Keith Raniere's initials burned into your flesh?" I would have run the other way. But twelve years later, by developing the support I needed to come forward and share what happened, I stopped more women from being branded. I'll never know how many women gained the information they needed to end their association with Keith Raniere because I, along with Mark, Bonnie, Nippy, and Catherine Oxenberg, had come forward with what we knew. Each of us, including Frank Parlato, Barry Meier, and many other journalists over the years have played an important role in exposing the darkness behind NXIVM's front of "personal development."

On Wednesday, June 19, 2019, after a six-week trial, a jury convicted Keith Raniere of all counts—racketeering and racketeering conspiracy; sex trafficking; attempted sex trafficking and sex trafficking conspiracy; forced labor conspiracy; and wire fraud conspiracy.

As these legal charges and verdicts unfolded, I was grieving two huge losses. One was my friendship with Lauren. We'd been close for twelve years, and I was devastated to see how she'd been used by Keith and her own mother for their personal gain. Lauren is a good person. Allegedly she and her mother were both Keith's lovers, and if that's true, I can't imagine how that's affected her. What I do know is the hurt I've felt because she can't pick up the phone and say, "I'm so sorry I lied to you about DOS." She flipped it around to make me look like a criminal to the loyalists who remained in the community. I know that much of that is part of her training in NXIVM: to protect Keith above all else. She admitted under oath that she lied to me, among others, for Keith's approval. That's the closure for me.

I also lost myself. My identity was so wrapped up in my community. All of that was severed in such a violent, sudden way when I finally put the pieces together and woke up. In helping others discover their power, I'm also rediscovering who I am and reclaiming myself and my own voice from a new vulnerable but authentic place. My true strength comes in being myself, a person who can make mistakes, make amends, and continue to evolve.

HEALING

VANCOUVER

Coming to terms with the fact that I was an unwitting part of a deceitful criminal enterprise is a challenging hurdle to get over. For months after figuring out that Keith was a sociopath, I couldn't sleep. I couldn't eat. I dropped a ton of weight. I was super-neurotic. I found that no matter how hard I tried to inhale and fill my lungs, I couldn't take a full breath. The panic was . . . well, visceral.

I was back on pills to help me sleep at night. I had extra locks installed in our house, like the ones on hotel-room doors. I only posted on social media days after I'd left a location, in case Keith wanted to track down where I was. That was the level of paranoia, because my opinion was that Keith Raniere seemed to have a strong determination to silence a woman when he wanted to. Call it dishonorable, but I have no doubt that Keith is a sociopath and needs to be locked up forever.

Very recently, for the first time in a year, I met for lunch with a friend in Vancouver who'd been part of our Ethos group. She'd been suffering an illness, but she was cagey about telling me about it because she thought I'd judge her. I took her hand. "It's OK, you can tell me," I said. "You aren't bad or wrong." It was painful for us to acknowledge this, but we'd been conditioned to believe that even our illnesses were brought on by our own choices; that getting sick was a parasitic method of seeking attention. Because in NXIVM, there are no victims. Injuries and ailments were said to be a manifestation of some deficiency. Since leaving NXIVM, I'm striving to be gentler and less judgmental of myself when I'm not feeling well, when I've made a mistake, or when things aren't going smoothly. Yes, with the aggressive tools, techniques, and practices in NXIVM, I had felt more in command of things, but the ranking system and overall structure created such insanity in my life, such disharmony in my relationships. It's not how I want to live anymore. "I'm so happy they caught him," I told Nippy right after Keith was arrested.

"Now we can live a normal life," Nippy said. "Just to go for hikes, to take our kid to the park. We can be a family. That's all I want."

I started to cry. My husband's saying this made me feel like finally I was off the hook. I didn't have to keep pushing, growing, advancing, or trying to be this superior, highly evolved human being. We could just live our life. Since we'd gotten married, this was all I'd wanted.

"See?" he said. "Now you're 'happy.'" His playfully sarcastic tone was reminiscent of our time in ESP, when a peer or coach would point out that when my "worlds had aligned" that my deficiency was covered up.

"No, Nippy," I said. "That's just being happy, and it's OK." That interaction was my first of many "post-ESP integrations" as I like to call them, where the programming has started to unwind. I realized right then that that is why so many devoted Espians in Albany appeared so miserable—Keith had programmed us to believe that happiness, or feeling good in any way, was actually bad. Now I was going to live my life and find true happiness and not feel bad or guilty about it. I'm learning to navigate everyday situations without second-guessing every emotion, and I understand that no person—not Keith Raniere, and not me—can know, do, or be everything. I don't put anyone on a pedestal anymore. No one can determine my worth.

On March 5, 2018, I sent a message to Lauren on the same message thread we'd been using a year earlier when I'd made the commitment to DOS. *Lauren,* I said, *I want you to know that Nippy and I were talking and it's not that we hate you. We feel badly for you. You didn't need to blackmail me to be a friend of yours for life. I*

*was already committed. You betrayed me on a massive level. BUT
I KNOW you have been betrayed too. Mostly I feel sad for you. But I
don't hate you.*

I signed off with a bright red heart.

Four days later, on the one-year anniversary of the branding, I
texted:

March 9ᵗʰ. It has been a year.

*I hope that you are doing some deep soul searching and
working hard to break your deep dependency on Keith. Go
back to your real dad. He is a good man. And find a real
boyfriend and have a child. Keith won't give you one. You
deserve it. And if you stop drinking the koolaid, You will
make a good mother. I really do hope you wake up . . . get
healthy and find your peace. This is for you Lauren.*

And I sent a link to the video for Kesha's song "Praying." The first
time I'd heard it, I cried as the words resonated so deeply as if they had
been written for Lauren and me. "You brought the flames and you put
me through hell. . . ." A reminder of what I have gone through, and a
recognition that I had indeed learned how to fight for myself. I played
the song over and over again, thinking of Lauren and praying for her
soul to heal too.

From the double checkmark on each message, I can see that she
read them both. But she's never responded. At least, not on purpose.
One day in March 2018, Lauren sent a text to Nippy, we think by accident, of a meme with a little girl wearing a crown that said: "Not everyone can be a princess. Someone has to wave when I go by."

"I'll wave to you when you're behind bars, Lauren," Nippy replied.

Today I see things from new angles; I understand the perspec-
tives of people who had questions about NXIVM. I continue to come
to terms with the friendships I've lost over the years; all the people I
chose not to pursue as friends and acquaintances because they weren't
interested in ESP. There were friends whose weddings I didn't go to
because it was an "ethical breach"—a betrayal of my own supposed

ethics—to choose a wedding over advancing in my NXIVM trainings. In 2015, my stepmother died of cancer just one month after she was diagnosed. We'd never properly made amends over our conflict about NXIVM, but sometimes I close my eyes and whisper to her: "You were right." It hurts me to know that I allowed NXIVM lies to come between us.

I can never go back and change the way I chose my priorities. I'm trying to take back my power and not give NXIVM all my energy . . . but the fact is, I will live the rest of my life with those regrets.

To deal with this and so much more, I'm working with a team of therapists who are helping me find tools to cope—a specialist in New York City who has expertise in cults and narcissistic sociopaths, a traditional psychologist, and a couples counselor. Still in mama bear mode, I've been helping others process, encouraging them to enter therapy too. And even though I've re-immersed myself in my career as an actor, I'm allowing the most important things in my life, my family, to bring me purpose. My son is four-and-a-half as I write this. Nippy and I had our second child in March 2019—two years after Lauren convinced me to be her slave. Less than two months later, Keith's trial got underway. Every single day for weeks, new details about DOS appeared in the court transcripts and headlines. One thing became clear: what we blew the whistle on was the tip of iceberg. Keith's abhorrent abuse of power ruined many people's lives— but that is their story to tell. I remained focused, completing this book to get the truth out, to reach other women by sharing my story, so that others will be inspired to come forward and speak their truth. The time of remaining silent is over! Some of us are also hoping to put together a class action lawsuit to help people who lost thousands of dollars in getting their money back.

I know my efforts are working. As Nancy, Lauren, Allison, and Clare stepped up one by one to plead guilty, I began to hear from other women who'd joined DOS or who had received the pitch to join. Writing me on email or WhatsApp from different areas of the U.S. and Mexico, these women apologized for having shunned me after I came forward to the media and FBI. They thanked me for my courage and for saving them from suffering the same fate I had, having narrowly missed getting branded. But what I least expected to learn was that I'd saved my dear friend. In her testimony, Lauren revealed that she was under real physical threat to do anything Keith demanded. Lauren publicly testified that over the years Keith had compelled her to have sex with many of the women we knew: Pam Cafritz, Barb J., Allison Mack, and others. I hope one day she will find herself and the happiness she was looking for when she committed herself to the Stripe Path and to Keith. I hope she can have a family and find peace. I don't know if we will ever be close again, but I hope she'll eventually understand the choice I made. I didn't just walk away quietly when I could have. The journey of trying to be who they wanted me to be led me to discover who I really am and what I'm really made of. This is me.

And what will stay with me forever, no matter how much scar cream I use, is my brand. My son sometimes asks me about my scar. "When's your boo-boo gonna get better, Mama?" If I have to live with this mark on my body for the rest of my life, I'll know that I did everything in my power to prevent any other women from having their bodies violated this way.

There is some quiet solace in all this, and that is the positive parts of NXIVM I've taken with me. Although it was through an unexpected and hellish experience, Keith Raniere was indeed a "master teacher who brought my issues to light." Don't get me wrong, I am not paying tribute to him. He was right about one thing: "character is only character when it's tested." By risking it all to end DOS and stop the continued abuse, I had an opportunity to become the type of person I've always wanted to be.

While Keith Raniere sits in prison, I hope he still believes that each of us causes everything that happens to us. I hope he is wondering how he created his situation. While he contemplates that, we'll use what he taught us—including the lessons we learned through the collapse of NXIVM—to live our best lives.

Healing after a betrayal takes time. It's a deep wound that can be easily reopened. Telling my story, albeit imperfectly, and doing what feels like the right thing, even in the face of great adversity, has been the best way for me to heal. I hope what I've learned will help others— how to spot danger, to avoid abusive relationships, to have the strength to leave, and to know that no matter what anyone else says, you are loved, you are whole, and you are already complete.

ACKNOWLEDGMENTS

This book could not have been written without the endless support from my family.

Thank you to my loving and handsome husband for feeding me, loving me, and helping me find my words in all this craziness. I can't imagine having gone through this process without you. You are a fantastic ally.

Thank you to my mom, who signed me up for a creative writing class and encouraged me to process. Thank you for cooking for me, holding the baby, and helping to put the kids to bed, so I could write. Most importantly, thank you for always keeping a lifeline to me, even though you knew what was going on behind the curtain.

Thank you to my dad, who has always inspired me to stand up for what I believe in, for your endless support with the kids—the sleepovers, the music, and the LEGO!

To my brother, who has always been younger but perhaps smarter—the best uncle my kids could ask for. Thank you for never judging me.

Thank you to my extended family, who always loved me even though they thought I was probably in a cult. And who welcomed me back with open arms when I saw the light. You know who you are.

To my friends who had my back, held my hand, made sure I was eating, and encouraged me to speak my truth. There are so many, but especially Meghan and Chris, Caroline and Pepe, Jenn and Jon, Jamie and Miguel, K'shin and Gaby, Chris and Maris, Paige, Diana, Erika, Tanya, and Wade for your kindness and friendship.

Special thank you to the original fire starter—Bonnie Piesse—who woke up first and to the silver fox—Mark Vicente—for getting me in and getting me out. And for doing the heavy lifting at the trial. You are a brave man.

Thank you: To Johnny for helping me to move the student files to the safety of my lawyers. To Nora for stepping in to help me with my children and my home, so I could focus on this book. To Steph for holding the babe and for taking care of us when we got back from the hospital. To Gary Harvey for giving me my first job back in reality. To Vasco for your discerning eye and kind heart. And to Andie MacDowell who told me, a few weeks after leaving NXIVM, that I would be "fine, just fine."

To my healers—Dr. John Pidutti for treating my scar and PTSD. To all of the cult experts—Rosanne Henry, Rick Ross, Steven Hassan, Janja Lalich, and especially Dan Shaw for your wisdom and compassion. All of you gave me perspective on cults and cultic structures, so that I can understand what I had been a part of. And thank you to my therapist, Dr. Noah Susswein, for your insights and for helping me to dismantle my programming and be happy again.

Thank you to Eckhart Tolle, who crossed my path at the perfect time and reminded me "not to throw the baby out with the bathwater." Thank you for showing me what spirituality without toxicity or ego looks like.

Thank you also to Adam Levine and your whole team at Verve—especially to my literary agent extraordinaire, Liz Parker, for your fabulous pep talks. Thank you to my agents of many years—Murray Gibson and Stacey Ando at Red Talent Management, and to Caroline Young and Annie Huang at the Characters. Thank you for not giving up on me.

Thank you to Josh Bloch and his whole team at the CBC for creating a space for me to tell my story with their powerful podcast.

Huge thank you to my intrepid editor Cara Bedick—your support as I figure out how to parent a five-year-old and a newborn while becoming a first-time author has meant the world to me. Your sensitivity to the issues surrounding my experience brought me much comfort. I am so grateful for your whole team at Chronicle Prism—Susan Amster, Eva Avery, Freesia Blizzard, Shona Burns, Dean Burrell, Pamela Geismar, Jennifer Jensen, Shelby Meizlik, Sara Schneider, Maureen Forys, and especially to Mark Tauber—you made me feel seen, heard, and valuable. Thank you for bringing my story to the world.

To Peter MacDougall and Jamie Broadhurst and everyone at Raincoast—thank you for your guidance, support, and enthusiasm in sharing my message.

To Krissy, who wholeheartedly went on this journey with me. Thank you for stepping into my crazy world to tell this story. It's important, and I couldn't have asked for a better guide. We found REAL female empowerment through this process, and I know we will be friends for life.

I don't have enough words to thank Moira Penza, Tanya Hajjar, Mark Lesko, Mike Weniger, Mike Lever, and Charlie Fontonelli. You have all poured so much energy and resources into this case, and your tenacity for truth truly makes the world a better place. I applaud all of you and your team at the DOJ and FBI.

To all of my lawyers—thank you for upholding justice! Neil Glazer, Zahra Dean on the East Coast, Ian Donaldson on the West coast. And Peter Skolnik and Mike Grygiel for your advice and support. I couldn't have done this without you!

Thank you in advance to anyone who reads this and thinks that I missed something or that something wasn't told accurately. Thank you for your patience. I have learned I can't please everyone—I am not perfect and I am OK with that now.

And thank you to all of the strangers who sent me letters of encouragement on social media. Thank you for telling me how going public has helped you. It motivated me when I didn't want to continue.

Thank you to everyone in our precious Vancouver ESP community—what we had was special, and I will cherish our time together always. Thank you to those who stayed close and who helped me pack up the center and clean up this mess in general.

To all of the people who believed me and trusted me, both "going in" and "going out." To the people who haven't woken up yet who will read this one day—I hope we will be friends again. To all the people who felt that I cut you out or in any way was not compassionate, please forgive me. I am so deeply sorry. I have always had good intentions and I hope you will know my true heart.

ABOUT THE AUTHOR

Sarah Edmondson is a Canadian actress and playwright who has starred in the CBS series *Salvation* and more than twelve films for the Hallmark Channel and Lifetime. She is also a well-established voice-over artist for popular series such as *Transformers: Cybertron* and *My Little Pony: Friendship Is Magic*. She is featured in the CBC podcast *Uncover: "Escaping NXIVM"* and *The Vow,* the upcoming HBO documentary series on NXIVM.

Kristine Gasbarre is the author of the memoir *How to Love an American Man,* as well as the co-writer of the #1 *New York Times* bestselling *Etched in Sand,* by Regina Calcaterra. Her work has been featured in such media outlets as *People, Glamour,* and the Oprah Winfrey Network.